SECTION 1
IN THE GARDEN

There's nothing quite like holding a bouquet of fresh herbs just picked from your own garden. Luscious basil, crisp parsley, and delicate chervil are just a few of the flavorful delights you can grow in containers on the porch steps or in a garden bed—even if you have never had your own garden before.

In this section, you will find the keys to growing fifteen essential herbs for your cooking and eating pleasure. For each herb, you will learn which varieties to buy, how to plant and grow them, and how to harvest for maximum flavor.

Growing herbs is as easy as 1 - 2 - 3:

1. Choose a place for your herbs where they will get three to four hours of direct sunlight.
2. Plant herbs in containers with premium potting soil or in fertile ground with good drainage.
3. Fertilize your herbs monthly in pots, less often in the ground.

The instructions in this book have been written with gardeners living in both warm and cool climates in mind, using the gardening temperature zone system developed by the United States Department of Agriculture to identify the areas where each herb is best grown. If you live outside North America, the USDA zones will not cover your location but can be used to help you understand how cold hardy each herb is and how best to grow it in your region.

IN THE GARDEN

BASIL

Who can resist the spicy aroma that wafts from basil on a warm sunny day in an herb garden? The fragrance will lure you closer to touch the leaves and release even more of the heady scent. Basil is sometimes called "the king of herbs," and it's easy to understand why. Whether in the garden or the kitchen, it commands our attention.

THE BASICS

Basil (*Ocimum basilicum*) is a warm weather annual herb with succulent and highly aromatic leaves growing in alternating pairs on upright square stems. Leaves vary from light green to dark purple and can be small as 1 inch (2.5 cm) or as large as 5 inches (12.5 cm) long. Most types of basil grow about 2 feet (61 cm) high and nearly as wide. During the height of summer, 4- to 6-inch (10 to 15 cm) stalks of small white to maroon flowers appear on the crown of this herb.

COMMON VARIETIES

The most popular basil is 'Sweet Green', which has bright green curved leaves. For the best pesto flavor, grow 'Genovese' or 'Mrs. Burns Lemon', two reliable producers in most regions. For an extra flavor kick, try 'Spicy Globe', which will

HOMEGROWN HERB GARDEN

LISA BAKER MORGAN
and ANN McCORMICK

A GUIDE TO GROWING AND COOKING DELICIOUS HERBS

CRESTLINE

Brimming with creative inspiration, how-to projects, and useful information to enrich your everyday life, Quarto Knows is a favorite destination for those pursuing their interests and passions. Visit our site and dig deeper with our books into your area of interest: Quarto Creates, Quarto Cooks, Quarto Homes, Quarto Lives, Quarto Drives, Quarto Explores, Quarto Gifts, or Quarto Kids.

This edition published in 2019 by Crestline,
an imprint of The Quarto Group
142 West 36th Street, 4th Floor
New York, NY 10018 USA
T (212) 779-4972 F (212) 779-6058
www.QuartoKnows.com

First published in 2015 by Quarry Books, an imprint of The Quarto Group,
100 Cummings Center Suite 265D, Beverly, MA 01915, USA.

Crestline titles are also available at discount for retail, wholesale, promotional, and bulk purchase. For details, contact the Special Sales Manager by email at specialsales@quarto.com or by mail at The Quarto Group, Attn: Special Sales Manager, 100 Cummings Center Suite 265D, Beverly, MA 01915, USA.

Design: Debbie Berne
Layout: Megan Jones Design
Photography: Alan De Herrera
Styling: Lisa Baker Morgan

10 9 8 7 6 5 4 3 2 1

ISBN: 978-0-7858-3721-3

Printed in China

FROM ANN: To Gene, my love, my friend, and my in-house editor.

FROM LISA: Dedicated to my family, living and passed, with love.

CONTENTS

II. IN THE KITCHEN 42

INTRODUCTION

THE GARDENER AND THE COOK

Passion for something brings with it an enthusiasm to do, a desire to learn, and the realization that despite what you know, there is always more to learn. Herein lies the story of this gardener and this chef, how this book began, and why this book is for all gardeners and cooks regardless of your level of experience.

It is a natural for someone who loves to cook to be curious about ingredients: their variations, where they come from, and how they are grown. The same can be said for someone who loves to garden. A gardener, sowing, growing, and experimenting with varieties is naturally desirous of new ways to use what has been cultivated. We are no exception. Both of us have pursued our respective interests, but we wanted to know more about the other's end of the process. This book is a fusion of our respective experience, knowledge, and talent. It is countless seasons of gardening and years of cooking school distilled into one book.

The book is divided into two sections, organized in the practical order of when you will use it. The first section of the book is devoted to gardening. The second section is devoted to cooking. For this first book, we chose the most widely used herbs and added a few that we are mad about but may be less familiar to you, such as chervil and Thai basil.

In "In the Garden," you will learn when to plant, where to plant, how and when to harvest your herbs, and how to dry and store those you don't use immediately in the kitchen.

In "In the Kitchen," you will learn about flavor pairings and how to use each herb in numerous ways in sweet and savory dishes and through the use of all cooking techniques.

Happily, we were able to satisfy our mutual curiosities and both of us have learned something about the other's expertise: Ann now knows what to do with chervil, which has

been less prevalent in the United States than in Europe, and Lisa knows why her Italian parsley grows strong while her basil flounders. We offer this book to you with the sincere hope that you will not only grow a range of herbs in your garden but also use those fresh herbs routinely in your cooking. We are confident that after reading this book you will be able to do just that and embellish on this foundation with great success. We will await your dinner invitation.

Happy planting.
Happy cooking.

ANN AND LISA

grow into a 2- to 3-foot (61 to 91 cm) hemisphere. Gardeners who enjoy Asian foods should grow Thai basil (A). The light green leaves on purple stems are excellent for stir-fry dishes. This is also one of the few types of basil with a large decorative flower cluster. If you make herbal vinegars, look for 'Purple Ruffles' or 'Red Rubin' (B). These varieties have deep red crinkly leaves that provide a ruby tint when steeped in vinegar.

CARE AND FEEDING

All types of basil grow best in full sun with warm temperatures and plenty of water. Don't set them out too early in the growing season. Wait until the soil and air temperatures are above 60°F (15.6°C) and all danger of frost is past. Find a spot with at least four hours of direct sunlight and mix organic amendments in with the soil to help hold moisture and give the plant a boost. Water basil regularly to maintain growth, but allow the soil to become dry to the touch between waterings to avoid damage to the roots through

overwatering. Spray with insecticidal soap as needed to combat chewing insects.

Since you're growing basil for the flavorful leaves, watch out for emerging flowers, which drain energy away from the desired leaf production. When daytime temperatures rise above 80°F (26.7°C), you'll see the stem tips begin to form a square cluster of four leaves layered tightly one on top of another. Your basil is reaching maturity and forming a flower spike.

The first impulse most gardeners have is to pinch off the tip. Deadheading, or pinching off the flower spike, doesn't halt the flowering—it simply makes way for the next flower stalk. Instead, cut at least six leaf nodes down the stem. Your basil will resume leaf production again, which is exactly what you want.

GROWING IN SMALL SPACES

Most basil needs a container at least 18 inches (45.7 cm) in diameter for

vigorous growth. If you are planting in smaller pots, look for small-leaf basils such as 'Windowbox' or 'Italian Cameo'. Don't plant small basil in large pots. The soil is likely to remain damp between waterings, encouraging fungus. Instead, keep the pot in proportion to the plant's size, transplanting it as it grows.

HARVESTING

Harvesting basil is the ultimate payoff to growing this luscious herb. Wait until the plant has reached at least 1 foot (30.5 cm) high before making your first cut. For the first harvest, cut stems just above the second set of leaves (counting from the bottom). New stems will form at this juncture. Basil should be harvested periodically during the summer. The more often you harvest basil, the better the flavor and the greater your total production will be.

DID YOU KNOW?

In the spring, if retailers are still keeping their basil in greenhouses, then it's too early for it to be planted outside in your garden.

Basil can be used as a mosquito repellent by either crushing the leaves or applying the oil to your skin.

Basil seeds can be fickle when it comes to germinating. The ancient Romans believed basil grew best if you cursed and screamed as you sowed the seeds.

IN THE GARDEN

BAY LAUREL

Very few trees are considered a proper part of an herb garden. Most herbs are annuals and small shrubby perennials. But there's one tree that stands tall in an herb garden of useful plants—bay laurel. Its tall spires of glossy leaves provide a fragrant focal point.

THE BASICS

The bay laurel tree (*Laurus nobilis*) is a multi-trunked tree growing to 40 feet (12.2 m) in its native region of Asia Minor. In North America and other northern regions, however, you're not likely to see one growing that large because cold winters limit the size. It sports 3- to 4-inch (7.5 to 10 cm) deep green glossy leaves that grow densely along the smooth-barked branches. When grown under ideal conditions, bay laurel will bloom in summer with pale yellow flowers.

COMMON VARIETIES

Although most nurseries carry just the traditional dark green-leaved bay laurel (A), there are varieties with light golden leaves, such as 'Aurea' and 'Sicilian Sunshine'. On the West Coast of the United States, bay laurel is sometimes confused with the native California or mountain laurel (*Umbellularia californica*). It has a similar flavor to bay laurel but contains essential oils that can cause headaches and may be toxic in sufficient concentration.

CARE AND FEEDING

Plant bay laurel in full sun where it will be protected from high winds and will have room to spread. It is a relatively shallow-rooted tree that will benefit from regular mulching. Bay laurel is a multi-trunked tree but can be trained to a more upright form by removing any secondary trunks. For the most part, it is a trouble-free plant that is rarely attacked by fungus or insects.

Bay laurel is definitely a warm-climate tree. It will grow reliably only as far north as Zone 8. When temperatures dip below freezing for any length of time, the leaves will turn a pale brown and drop off. If freezing weather is predicted, a cloth covering and mulch at the base can make all the difference between life and death. If you live in colder regions, plant bay laurel in a large pot so you can bring it indoors for winter protection. Water sparingly during winter—just enough so it doesn't dry out.

GROWING IN SMALL SPACES

Gardeners with limited space can easily grow bay laurel in a container. Plant it in a pot at least 18 inches (45.7 cm) deep to provide adequate room for roots. Bay laurel tends to grow more slowly in a pot than in the ground. Fertilize monthly to encourage growth. Overwinter bay laurel under protection or bring indoors during the winter if your area is subject to below-freezing temperatures.

HARVESTING

The leaves of bay laurel can be clipped anytime for fresh use. Use leaves no more than six months old. Anything older than that will be less flavorful.

A

DID YOU KNOW?

Always remove bay laurel leaves from foods before serving. Even after cooking the leaves remain stiff and can get caught in the throat if accidentally swallowed.

Crowns of laurel leaves were awarded to winning athletes at the ancient Greek Olympic Games.

The priestesses in ancient Delphi chewed leaves of bay laurel to evoke a religious trance and stimulate visions of the future.

IN THE GARDEN

CHERVIL

If you have a shady spot in your garden (and who doesn't?), then you have the perfect place to grow chervil. This cheerful herb sports attractive feathery leaves that just beg to be touched and enjoyed, releasing their refreshing anise scent.

THE BASICS

Chervil (*Anthriscus cerefolium*) is a member of the parsley family that can be successfully grown in Zone 3 and warmer. Like parsley, this short-lived herb grows in a 1- to 2-foot (30.5 to 61 cm)-tall clump of leafy stems, but the light green leaves with hints of silver are more finely divided than those of parsley. Some say chervil resembles a small fern, making it a good edible to grow side by side with ornamental flowers. In early summer, chervil sends up flat-topped, umbrella-shaped flower heads of tiny white flowers that can be clipped and dried for everlasting arrangements.

COMMON VARIETIES

When purchasing, look for the 'Crispum' variety, which has curly leaves. You also might see 'Brussels Winter' chervil, which grows taller than common chervil and tolerates warmer temperatures before bolting.

Don't confuse true chervil with 'Sweet' or 'Spanish' chervil (*Myrrhis odorata*), also known as sweet cicely, which grows twice as tall as chervil and has a more pronounced anise flavor.

CARE AND FEEDING

Chervil should be planted in full sun when grown in cooler regions. It can be finicky about being moved. Sow seeds directly in place to avoid transplanting problems. Allow two weeks for them to germinate. Once they are 3 to 4 inches (7.5 to 10 cm) high, thin the young plants to about 10 inches (25.4 cm) apart. Whether as seeds or transplants, chervil should be placed where the roots will get plenty of moisture. Water regularly and fertilize about every six weeks to encourage healthy growth.

Chervil is a tender annual in warmer regions and will not withstand extreme summer heat. Gardeners in these regions should plant it early in the year, as soon as the danger of frost has passed. Once the daytime highs get above 100°F (37.8°C), chervil is likely to set seed and die. The wise gardener accepts this and plants more chervil after the heat of summer begins to fade. If you give this second sowing of herb protection from early frosts, it may last until Christmas.

GROWING IN SMALL SPACES

Chervil will grow nicely in containers along with other herbs. Gardeners in Zone 7 and warmer should place their potted chervil in dappled to full shade to minimize problems with bolting. This is also one of the few culinary herbs that will tolerate low-light conditions and can be successfully grown indoors.

HARVESTING

Chervil can be harvested about six to eight weeks after seeds have germinated. Clip the outer stems and allow the inner leaves to grow and mature. Chervil, like cilantro, is best used fresh but can also be flash-frozen for off-season use.

DID YOU KNOW?

Too much sun or warm temperatures will spur chervil to set seed and die.

Chervil is one of the four herbs in the French seasoning blend "fines herbes." The others are parsley, chive, and tarragon.

In the region from Quebec to Pennsylvania, chervil has escaped cultivated gardens and become naturalized.

IN THE GARDEN
CILANTRO

One of the benefits of growing cilantro is discovering how flavorful it can be when picked fresh. It is a must-have herb when making guacamole, pico de gallo, and many other spicy foods we have adopted from our neighbors to the south.

THE BASICS

Cilantro (*Coriandrum sativum*) is a short-lived cool weather annual herb that grows 12 to 18 inches (30.5 to 45.7 cm) high and slightly more than 12 inches (30.5 cm) wide. In the early stages of its life cycle, it produces medium green, finely divided leaves on stalks that rise from a central base. Later in life, as the weather warms, it sends up a central flower stalk, which produces umbrella-shaped flower heads of tiny white to pink flowers and eventually forms the seeds we call coriander.

COMMON VARIETIES

Since most gardeners want to maximize the amount of cilantro they harvest, look for "slow-bolt" varieties, which will increase production by two to three weeks. Recent introductions include 'Calypso' and 'Marino' cilantro. Take care not to confuse this herb with culantro (*Eryngium foetidum*), a Caribbean herb with prickly, strap-shaped leaves and a flavor similar to but definitely stronger than cilantro.

CARE AND FEEDING

Cilantro seeds can be sown in late winter directly in the soil where you want them. Allow two weeks for seeds to germinate, especially in cold weather. Thin seedlings so they are 8 to 10 inches (20.3 to 25.4 cm) apart. If you purchase young cilantro plants, take care to avoid damage to the central taproot when you transplant them. Water regularly and fertilize about every six weeks to encourage healthy growth.

In hot climates, cilantro needs to be treated like a two-season annual. The first season for cilantro is late winter through early summer. Cilantro produces flavorful leaves during the cooler spring days. But when temperatures exceed 90°F (32.2°C), leaf production stops as it bolts, sets seed, and dies. The remains of the cilantro plant should be pulled up and discarded. Then, around early fall, warm climate gardeners should plant a second crop of this spicy herb. As temperatures cool, these new cilantro plants will grow happily until winter frost ends production.

In regions with high humidity, watch for powdery mildew or leaf spot. You can prevent these problems by placing cilantro where it will get good air circulation. If the problem persists, remove the leaves most affected and use antifungal powder.

GROWING IN SMALL SPACES

Cilantro will grow just fine in raised beds or small rooftop gardens. Warm climate gardeners can take advantage of a container garden's mobility by moving it to cool locations in late spring to delay bolting.

HARVESTING

You can begin harvesting cilantro about five weeks after transplanting. Leaves are clipped from the outer area of the plant to allow the inner core to mature. Continue harvesting until the central flower stalk appears. Once that happens, the leaves become less flavorful.

Cilantro leaves lose much of their flavor when they are dried. Instead, try freezing the leaves to retain flavor. The ripe seeds (aka coriander) can be easily dried and stored as you would other seed herbs.

DID YOU KNOW?

In the produce section of Asian food markets, you'll sometimes find cilantro labeled as "Chinese parsley."

The Latin name *coriandrum* has its roots in the Greek word for "bedbug," memorializing the unfortunate aromatic similarity between the plant and the insect.

In the "language of flowers," cilantro symbolizes "hidden merit."

IN THE GARDEN

DILL

When we think of delicious seafood–salmon, shrimp, mussels–we naturally think of dill. The flavor of this herb goes well with anything harvested from the ocean. Added to butters or sauces, the light green feathery leaves provide the perfect flavor complement to these dishes.

THE BASICS

Dill (*Anethum graveolens*) is a tall annual herb that can grow as far north as Zone 2. It forms thick, hollow stalks that rise rapidly to 4 feet (1.2 m) or more. The medium green leaves are composed of thin, lacy strands. It grows best in full sun with regular watering. In summer, it produces umbrella-shaped clusters of tiny white flowers that ripen into light brown dill seeds.

COMMON VARIETIES

'Bouquet' dill grows to about 3 feet (91.4 cm), blooms early, and produces large seed heads. This is the variety to plant for gardeners who harvest the seeds to make their own pickles. 'Fernleaf' dill is slow to set seed, grows only 18 inches (45.7 cm) tall, and is a good choice for planting with ornamental flowers. 'Dukat' dill grows to about 2 feet (61 cm) tall. It is grown for its blue-green foliage, which can be included in salads. This variety of dill is reported to have a higher essential oil content (the substance that gives herbs their flavor) but a more mellow taste than other dills.

CARE AND FEEDING

Although you can start the seeds of dill in pots indoors before setting them out in your garden, it's much simpler to sow them in place in mid-spring once daytime highs are firmly above 60°F (15.6°C). They will germinate easily, and you won't have the task of transplanting. Dill can be sown outdoors early in the growing year—as soon as overnight lows remain above freezing. Gardeners in hot climates (where dill will quickly go to seed) may find it helpful to sow a little dill every three to four weeks to ensure a steady supply of the fresh leaves.

Dill doesn't like competition, so it needs regular weeding to keep the plant healthy. In the border garden, plant dill in the rear so the tall stalks won't hide other plants. Grow it near a bay tree or other dark-leafed herb where the finely cut leaves will provide an interesting contrast.

Dill reseeds with the slightest wind. Wherever you sow it, be prepared to have dill growing there for years to come. Clip off the flower heads (A) when they appear to forestall reseeding. Disease is rarely a problem with dill. The biggest danger is from aphids, which attack the seed heads. Application of insecticidal soap should keep this under control.

GROWING IN SMALL SPACES

Dill grows a long central taproot, so it's unhappy in shallow containers.

Plant dill in pots at least 10 inches (25.4 cm) deep. Look for dwarf varieties such as 'Bouquet' and 'Fernleaf' if you have limited space.

HARVESTING

Dill leaves are best harvested just before use. Clip no more than 20 percent of available leaves at one time. Although clipped leaves can be refrigerated, they'll wilt and lose flavor quickly. If you choose to dry dill leaves, avoid using heat to speed the drying process because the leaves will lose too much flavor. Harvest dill seeds as soon as they turn brown.

DID YOU KNOW?

Dill flowers attract beneficial insects that prey on harmful sucking insects. They are also a host plant for butterfly caterpillars.

Dill was once known as "meeting seeds" because they would be taken to church meetings and slipped to small children to keep them quiet.

Old folk wisdom says that hanging dill by the front door will protect the home against witches and evil spirits.

IN THE GARDEN

FRENCH TARRAGON

Summer is the season of salads, picnics, and barbecues. For these "easy living" foods, nothing beats the unforgettable flavor of French tarragon. The fresh-picked leaves of this herb added to your kitchen creations will have your family and friends saying, "Ooh la la!"

THE BASICS

French tarragon (*Artemisia dracunculus*) is a pungent, low-growing herb with smooth, needlelike leaves. A perennial herb, it will thrive in a wide range of conditions, growing reliably as far north as Zone 4. It can also grow in hot, dry areas with as

little as 12 inches (30.5 cm) of annual rainfall. The thin stems are covered with long, narrow leaves and reach 1 to 3 feet (30.5 to 91.4 cm) high. In midsummer, French tarragon forms tiny greenish white blossoms, but the seeds they produce are sterile and will not germinate.

COMMON VARIETIES

When shopping for French tarragon, keep in mind that there are two herbs called tarragon, probably stemming from the same parent plant. The dark green French tarragon, which provides the best flavor in foods, is a sterile hybrid and can only be propagated by cuttings or division. The rough-leaved, lighter colored Russian tarragon (*Artemisia dracunculus dracunculoides*), the supposed parent of French tarragon, can be grown from seed but is coarser in flavor. If you find a packet of seeds labeled "tarragon," it is the less desirable Russian variety, so don't waste your money.

French tarragon does not grow well in regions with high humidity or poor air circulation. Gardeners in the humid United States Gulf Coast area may see an unrelated plant for sale called Texas tarragon or Mexican mint marigold (*Tagetes lucida*). It is a good substitute, providing a slightly sweeter but similar flavor.

CARE AND FEEDING

French tarragon is a generally resilient herb. It does not, however, grow well if subject to high humidity, poor drainage, or poor air circulation. Plant French tarragon in soil that is well drained—a sloped area or raised bed will work fine. Space young plants about 12 inches (30.5 cm) apart and fertilize. Around midsummer, give French tarragon a trim, cutting it back to about half its height. Mulch after the first winter frost to preserve the herb through the cold months.

Divide French tarragon every three to five years to maintain healthy growth. In early spring, dig up the dormant herb. Using a sharp knife, divide it into sections and replant.

GROWING IN SMALL SPACES

French tarragon is a compact herb that can be easily grown in small gardens or containers. Regular clipping will help maintain its compact shape.

HARVESTING

Clip fresh French tarragon anytime during the growing season. In fall, clip about half of the plant for drying. The flavor of French tarragon can also be preserved by steeping it in wine vinegar for year-round enjoyment.

DID YOU KNOW?

The Latin name *dracunculus* means "little dragon," referring to the tightly coiled roots of this herb.

In the "language of flowers," French tarragon symbolizes "unselfish sharing" or "lasting interest."

French tarragon is one of the few culinary herbs that is not used in herbal medicine.

IN THE GARDEN

ITALIAN PARSLEY

Every garden needs plants that are reliable performers in all kinds of weather. Parsley will fill this role in your herb garden. It's also a great performer in the kitchen, with its knack for helping other flavors blend into a pleasing whole.

THE BASICS

Italian parsley (*Petroselinum crispum*) is a biennial herb, meaning it grows for just two years. The first year it produces a bushy rosette of flavorful, long-stemmed dark green leaves that grow about 12 inches (30.5 cm) high. The second year, the leaves lose flavor and a 2- to 3-foot (61 to 91.4 cm) flower stalk rises from the center of the plant. The small white flowers produce nectar that is enjoyed by butterflies. A native of the cliff sides and rocky hills of Europe, parsley is hardy to Zone 4, provided the ground doesn't freeze, but it can be grown with protection as far north as Zone 2.

COMMON VARIETIES

When shopping for parsley in nurseries, you'll usually find two varieties—curly parsley (A) and flat-leafed Italian parsley (B). Both provide flavor, but cooks prefer the darker Italian parsley for its superior taste.

Occasionally, you may come across a third variety known as Hamburg parsley (*Petroselinum crispum tuberosum*). This parsley is grown for its large edible root, not the leaves.

CARE AND FEEDING

In early spring, plant Italian parsley in full sun to part shade. Space plants about 12 inches (30.5 cm) apart. Keep in mind that parsley has a long taproot (like its relative, the carrot) and will not be happy being transplanted. Parsley is susceptible to subterranean carrot weevils, so avoid planting it where you've grown carrots or other root crops in recent years.

Because parsley grows very differently in the first and second year of life, you have two options when positioning it in your garden. If you plan to keep it only one year for the leaves, grow it near other showy herbs or ornamentals as an edging or a border plant. But if you're willing to let it go to flower and attract butterflies the second year, plant it in the back of your bed to accommodate the tall flower stalk.

Keep parsley regularly watered to ensure healthy growth. Fertilize two or three times a year when grown in the ground or monthly when grown in containers. If you see evidence of insect damage, spray with insecticidal soap.

GROWING IN SMALL SPACES

Italian parsley is the perfect "starter plant" for someone planting their first container of herbs. It tolerates a wide range of conditions and grows reliably for the novice and the expert. Put it in a container at least 8 inches (20.3 cm) deep to give the roots plenty of room. Combine it with basil and onion chives for a wonderful trio of textures and flavors.

HARVESTING

Clip up to a third of the plant's leaves when harvesting. Make the cut about 2 inches (5 cm) from the ground. Parsley is one herb you really should use fresh. It tends to lose flavor when dried. As an alternative to drying parsley, you might try freezing the leaves for better flavor.

DID YOU KNOW?

Parsley is high in vitamins A, B_1, B_2, and C; niacin; calcium; and iron.

At the grocers, don't get Italian parsley confused with Chinese parsley, which is another name for cilantro.

Tradition says that parsley grows best in a garden where the woman of the house is the boss.

IN THE GARDEN

LEMONGRASS

If you enjoy making foods from Southeast Asia, you will want to grow lemongrass. The tender portions of this aromatic grass provide a light lemon flavor used in teas, soups, and stir-fry dishes.

THE BASICS

Lemongrass (*Cymbopogon citratus*) grows in clumps of tightly wrapped leaves with a bulbous base. The inner core is pale green and tender, somewhat resembling the lower part of a green onion. The light green, strap-shaped leaves are finely serrated (A). Lemongrass generally grows about 3 feet (91.4 cm) high, although it may grow to 6 feet (1.8 m) in ideal conditions. The overall effect in a garden is a gently rustling fountain of green, a nice contrast to other herbs. When grown in its native Asian tropics, it sends up a large, loose, compound flower head, but this is rarely seen when it is grown in more temperate climates.

CARE AND FEEDING

Because it is native to the tropics of Southeast Asia, lemongrass is regarded as a tender perennial in the continental United States and similar climates. It is hardy only in Zones 10 and 11, but it will survive mild winters with brief frosts. If your area gets hard frosts in the winter, you will need to grow it in a large container that can be brought in for the winter. Once indoors, regular misting helps control attacks of spider mites, a common problem with overwintering herbs.

Always use gloves when handling lemongrass. The fine serration on the edges of the leaves can cut you before you know it. Lemongrass has also been known in rare cases to cause contact dermatitis (itching or reddening of the skin and even blisters), another good reason for those gloves.

Lemongrass is propagated by division. A group of the tight cylindrical clumps of leaves can be separated from the main cluster for transplanting. Leave room for it to spread up to 2 feet (61 cm) in a year.

Lemongrass needs little care and is rarely attacked by insects. Like most shallow-rooted grasses, it enjoys having regular water, but once established, it can manage just fine on occasional rain.

In late fall, trim your clump to about 6 inches (15.2 cm) from the ground. This will remove the leaves, which will look a bit tattered from the weather. Dead areas in the middle of the clump are your cue that it is time to divide and replant the lemongrass. If your area is subject to unexpected low temperatures in winter, then heavily mulch lemongrass to help it survive brief frosts.

GROWING IN SMALL SPACES

Because of its size and frost sensitivity, most gardeners will find that lemongrass grows best in a large container. Plant your lemongrass in a pot at least 18 inches (45.7 cm) deep and place it where it will enjoy full sun. Water deeply and regularly. At the first sign of frost, bring lemongrass indoors for protection through the winter.

HARVESTING

To harvest, use your gloved hand to grab several leaf clusters that are at least $\frac{1}{2}$ inch (1.3 cm) in diameter at the base. Using a hand shovel or garden saw to assist, remove them from the main clump. Clip off all but 8 inches (20.3 cm) of the leaf base, discarding the tougher, less flavorful green leaves.

Freshly harvested lemongrass can be used immediately in foods or beverages. However, if you are harvesting in advance, lemongrass clusters can be stored for up to two weeks in the refrigerator in a glass of water to keep them crisp.

DID YOU KNOW?

Lemongrass is the only edible member of a family of aromatic grasses from southern India and Sri Lanka. It is a close cousin to citronella grass (*Cymbopogon nardus*), which yields mosquito-repelling citronella oil.

Lemongrass has been used medicinally on the Indian subcontinent for children's digestive problems, minor fevers, and certain skin diseases.

Lemongrass's antiseptic and antibacterial properties make it valuable in perfumes, soaps, hair products, and other cosmetics.

IN THE GARDEN
MINT

Of all the herbs I grow, none is more likely to evoke happy memories of childhood than mint. The smell and taste of this herb reminds me of my grandmother's garden and my first nibble of its fresh leaves. Now that I'm all grown up, I know that mint is just as wonderful in the kitchen as it is in the herb garden.

THE BASICS

Mint is a family of pungent herbs hardy to Zone 5. Mint leaves are 1 to 2 inches (2.5 to 5 cm) long and vary in color from deep green to golden to creamy variegated. Most mints grow about 12 inches (30.5 cm) high but spread out quickly by horizontal runners, or stolons. In early summer, some mints sport clusters of very tiny white flowers that attract bees.

COMMON VARIETIES

There's more to the mint world than just the ever-popular peppermint (*Mentha* x *piperita*) (A) and spearmint (*Mentha spicata*) (B). Pineapple mint (*Mentha suaveolens* var. *suaveolens*) (C) has lovely dark green fuzzy leaves edged with white. Apple mint (*Mentha suaveolens*) (D) has light green, oval, hairy leaves with stems growing 18 to 24 inches (45.7 to 61 cm) high. Curly mint (also known as 'Doublemint' for its familiar flavor) has dark green ruffled leaves.

CARE AND FEEDING

Most mints are native to streamsides, so in the garden, they like lots of water. Plant mint in full sun to part shade. Mint is best placed somewhere you can easily clip back the stolons and prevent them from appearing in the lawn or other unwanted spots. For the best flavor when you harvest, provide a high-nitrogen fertilizer in spring and late summer.

Mint is notorious for taking over a garden bed. This herb sends out stolons that burrow just under the soil's surface and can spread rapidly. Be sure to check mint every time you weed for those sneaky runners it constantly sends out. Pull them up and clip them off.

Mint is a favorite home for slugs and snails. Sprinkle snail bait or diatomaceous earth in your mint beds to discourage these pests. It also benefits from a severe trimming down to ground level in late fall. This prevents harmful insects from finding a winter home among the leaves and removes anything that could harbor the spores of damaging fungus.

In most areas, mint goes dormant and almost disappears during the winter months. If you live in an area with hard freezes, add a layer of mulch to protect the roots, and you'll have a lush, green bed of this herb when spring comes.

GROWING IN SMALL SPACES

Because of mint's invasive nature, gardeners with limited space should grow it in containers where its wanderlust can be kept in check. But even in a container, mint can be a problem as it crowds out its neighbors. Horizontal runners, denied access to distant locations, will circle the rim of the pot, seeking a way out. Each spring, dig up the entire plant and, using a sharp knife or shears, reduce the mint to a manageable segment. Tease apart the sections remaining and replant. You will have a rejuvenated mint and space for other herbs in the pot.

HARVESTING

Anytime is the right time to clip a sprig of mint and add it to iced tea and fruit dishes or use it as a garnish. For large-scale harvesting, it is best to cut mint in late summer, about the same time it flowers. This is when the essential oil content, which provides flavor, is at its peak.

DID YOU KNOW?

Don't waste your money on mint seeds. Most popular mints are sterile hybrids and can't be grown from seed.

Teach children about how roots grow by placing a mint cutting in a small vase in your kitchen window.

Mint has been used for centuries to settle the stomach and relieve abdominal cramps.

IN THE GARDEN

ONION CHIVES

The perky leaves and lavender flowers of onion chives are guaranteed to make you smile. They're fun to grow in garden beds or containers and are just as much fun to use in the kitchen.

THE BASICS

Onion chives (*Allium schoenoprasum*), a somewhat grassy herb, form tight clumps of onionlike bulbets. The plant is hardy in Zones 3 through 9 and grows about 12 inches (30.5 cm) tall with hollow, tubular leaves. In the spring, it produces lavender pompom flower heads. Onion chives are regarded as a semi-hardy perennial.

In regions with hard frost in winter, the plant will die down to the ground but quickly return in spring.

Onion chives like full sun and regular water. In regions where summers are exceptionally hot, plant it in an area where it will get shade during the heat of the day.

COMMON VARIETIES

When purchasing, check the plant label to see whether you're getting onion chives, which is what most cooks use, not garlic chives (*Allium tuberosum*), which are more commonly used in Asian cooking. When young, these botanical siblings look nearly identical. If the label is missing or vague, pick up the pot and take a sniff. The aroma of onion or garlic will reveal which one you have.

CARE AND FEEDING

Anytime during the growing season is the perfect time to plant this tender perennial herb. When purchasing, select a potted plant with as many young shoots as possible. They can easily be pulled apart and divided when transplanting, giving the seedlings more room to grow and multiplying your harvest. Keep well watered, especially in hot weather, to maintain the plant's health and ensure new leaves.

Plant onion chives anywhere you have full sun to part shade and good drainage. Garden spots that tend to stay soggy after a hard rain will eventually rot the bulbous roots.

Onion chives are rarely affected by pests or fungus. If they become over-stressed, aphids may attack. A quick application of insecticidal soap and eliminating the stressful conditions will correct this nicely.

The light green leaves and vertical growth of onion chives provide a nice contrast to the bushy shape of most herbs. Onion chives can also be tucked near ornamental flowers where their lavender blooms (A) will be admired, which appear in late spring to early summer.

The only problem with growing onion chives is their ability to self-sow, which often means an abundance of seedlings within a 3-foot (91.4 cm) radius of the main planting each spring. Fortunately, they can be pulled up with ease or passed on to fellow gardeners.

GROWING IN SMALL SPACES

Onion chives are content to grow in containers or pocket gardens as long as they have full sun and regular water. The plant's vertical growth adds visual interest when planted with other small-leaved herbs, such as thyme and sweet marjoram. In cold regions, onion chives can be potted and brought indoors for occasional harvest during the winter.

HARVESTING

Onion chives can be harvested as soon as the leaves reach about 6 inches (15.2 cm) high. Clip a section of onion chive leaves to about 2 inches (5 cm) above the ground. Regular cutting encourages this herb to spread and form new bulbets.

This is one of the few herbs that doesn't dry well because it loses much of its flavor in the process. Instead, clip and use fresh chives anytime during the year. Alternatively, you can harvest onion chives, snip the leaves into short sections, and freeze them for later use.

DID YOU KNOW?

Onion chive blossoms are edible and can be broken apart and sprinkled on salad for a flavorful gourmet touch.

Tradition says that Marco Polo introduced onion chives, a native of China, to cooks in Europe.

Onion chives contain many of the same heart-healthy phytochemicals as garlic.

IN THE GARDEN

ROSEMARY

Rosemary is a wonderfully aromatic shrub that should be in every herb garden. Its presence is equally dramatic in the kitchen, where it will transform any dish into a masterpiece of flavor.

THE BASICS

Rosemary (*Rosmarinus officinalis*) is a perennial shrub hardy to Zone 7. The slightly sticky, needle-shaped leaves are glossy dark green above and gray-green below. Small white, pink, or sky blue flowers appear in spring. With its sturdy branches, rosemary can grow to 6 feet (1.8 m) tall and nearly as wide if left unchecked, so give it room wherever you plant it.

COMMON VARIETIES

Rosemary has some great varieties available in nurseries. 'Majorca Pink' (A) has soft green leaves with lavender-pink flowers. 'Tuscan Blue' (B) has a distinctive upright habit with sky blue flowers. 'Prostrate' rosemary trails nicely and can withstand dry conditions on retaining walls or in rock gardens. Gardeners living in cold areas who have had trouble overwintering rosemary should look for 'Arp' or 'Madalene Hill' varieties. For something with a different look, try 'Golden Rain', which has dark blue flowers and golden leaves with a green center. These are just a few of the dozens of cultivars available. All are flavorful in the kitchen, so look around for one that will be pleasing to the eye as well as the palate.

CARE AND FEEDING

Plant rosemary where it will have good drainage and full sun for at least half of the day. This shrub has roots that will not tolerate wet conditions. The most common reason for dieback (loss of sections of the shrub) or death is overwatering, whether the condition is man-made or natural. Because rosemary likes things hot and dry, winters can be a problem for this evergreen. To improve survival in cold areas, plant rosemary in an area sheltered from harsh winter winds and add 2 to 3 inches (5 to 7.5 cm) of mulch in the fall.

Of all the herbs most commonly grown, rosemary is the one most likely to outgrow its location and become a problem. Lightly prune your rosemary in spring and late fall. If it is cut back too severely, though, it will fail to regrow and die. To avoid this, go easy as your trim. Don't cut branches down to where there are no leaves. Bare branches will not re-bud.

Rosemary is susceptible to attack from several pests, including spider mites, mealybugs, whiteflies, and thrips. A plant stressed from too much watering or high humidity is more vulnerable to these infestations. If these pests appear, trim back the sections heavily infested and spray the remaining areas with insecticidal soap.

GROWING IN SMALL SPACES

Rosemary is a shrub, so most varieties require frequent pruning to maintain a small size for containers. The one happy exception is 'Prostrate' rosemary. This is the ideal variety to plant in containers or hanging baskets. It maintains a small size and will cascade beautifully over the side.

HARVESTING

For immediate use of rosemary in cooking, clip 6-inch (15.2 cm) sections of recent growth. The newer the leaves, the better the flavor. Rosemary can be harvested year-round for drying. Once branches of rosemary are dried, remove the leaves by pinching the tip and moving your fingers down the stem. Your fingers will get sticky from the resin, so be prepared for a good scrubbing when you're done.

DID YOU KNOW?

Some of the essential oils in rosemary are the same as those in pine trees, making rosemary great for Christmas decorations.

Shakespeare's declaration that "rosemary is for remembrance" has been confirmed by modern scientific research. The scent of rosemary stimulates brain activity and enhances memory.

For centuries, bridesmaids carried rosemary during the wedding ceremony to symbolize their desire that the happy couple would remember the day and their vows with joy.

IN THE GARDEN

SAGE

There is something earthy and comforting about sage. In the garden, the thick, nubby leaves of sage will make a pleasing contrast with its neighbors. In the kitchen, the aroma will bring memories of holiday feasts with friends and family.

THE BASICS

Sage (*Salvia officinalis*) is a gray-green hardy perennial native to the Mediterranean, from Spain to Turkey. Depending on the variety, sage will grow from 1 to 4 feet (30.5 to 122 cm) tall. The thick oval leaves are 2 to 3 inches (5 to 7.5 cm) long with a pebbly texture. In late spring, spikes of sky-blue flowers appear above the leaves. Sage prefers full sun and relatively dry conditions. It is hardy to Zone 6 with protection from frost.

COMMON VARIETIES

An attractive variety of sage to appear recently is 'Silver Leaf'. It grows the same size as traditional sage but the leaves are a bit narrower and have more of a silver-gray color. Another favorite on the market is 'Berggarten'. The large leaves are more oval shaped and grow compactly on short stems. You'll also see 'Golden', 'Purpurea', and 'Tricolor' sages in nurseries. Although they are attractive in the garden, these three sages are not hardy north of Zone 8 and don't have the best flavor in the kitchen.

CARE AND FEEDING

Because it is native to dry, rocky areas of the Mediterranean, sage needs soil with fast drainage. Space young plants about 18 inches (45.7 cm) apart, where they will receive plenty of sunlight. Pair sage with darker-colored herbs such as rosemary for color contrast. 'Golden' sage and 'Tricolor' sage are less hardy in hot climates, so plant them where they will enjoy some shade.

Sage likes relatively dry conditions, so plant it in dry garden spots that don't get much moisture. Don't overwater your sage. Too much water is the biggest cause of this herb's death. Also avoid using sprinklers on them because this encourages spider mites to set up home in the plant's interior. Combat any infestation with a light pruning and insecticidal soap.

Most sage plants will last for three to four years. To maintain health and encourage leaf production, clip sage back in early spring and fall. Eventually, your sage will develop a dead area in the center. When that happens, it is time to divide. In early fall, dig up the entire plant. With a sharp garden saw or knife, divide the clump into three or four sections, removing any dead areas in the process. Replant the new sections at least 18 inches (45.7 cm) apart and water to establish the roots.

GROWING IN SMALL SPACES

Because of its compact growth habits, sage can be successfully grown by those with limited garden space—just prune periodically to maintain its small size. Sage will also grow in containers provided it is paired with other plants that have low-moisture needs.

HARVESTING

Clip sections of sage from the bush and then remove leaves from the stems to hasten drying. The thick leaves of sage take longer to dry than most herbs.

DID YOU KNOW?

Tradition says that drinking sage tea encourages health and long life.

In medieval England, sage was used in ale brewing and cheese making.

Sage was once so valued by the Chinese that it was accepted in trade for Chinese tea.

IN THE GARDEN

SWEET MARJORAM

Sweet marjoram is the "sleeper" of the culinary herb garden. It grows quietly among the other herbs, not drawing attention to itself, only to reach the kitchen and blow away the competition. Sweet marjoram has a mild, sweet flavor that chefs prefer to the more commonly used oregano. If you grow and cook with herbs, you should definitely have this in your garden.

THE BASICS

Sweet marjoram (*Origanum majorana*) is a tender perennial herb native to the Mediterranean. It grows reliably in Zones 9 to 11 but will survive in cooler regions if given winter protection. This herb produces a dense cluster of stems 1 to 2 feet (30.5 to 61 cm) high. Clusters of tiny white flowers appear in summer.

COMMON VARIETIES

Sweet marjoram is sometimes confused with oregano (*Origanum vulgare*), which is a different species altogether and less flavorful in the kitchen. Sweet marjoram has broad, almost heart-shaped leaves that are relatively smooth. Oregano leaves are narrower and lance shaped, with a somewhat downy appearance. When sweet marjoram is crossed with oregano, it produces 'Hardy Sweet' marjoram (*Origanum* x *majoricum*), which is sometimes labeled "Italian oregano."

CARE AND FEEDING

Position sweet marjoram near the front of your garden bed in an area with good drainage. Place plants about 12 inches (30.5 cm) apart. Because sweet marjoram is a tender herb, plant it where it will be sheltered from harsh winds. It will also benefit from nearby warmth radiated from stone or brick walls. Gardeners living in cold climates (north of Zone 6) should treat sweet marjoram as an annual and replant it every year.

Sweet marjoram will grow in full sun to part shade. The density of the leaves on the stem depends on the amount of direct sunlight the plant receives. Marjoram growing in a full-sun garden will have dark colored short stems with leaves tightly clustered together. If planted in a shade garden, it will have lighter colored stems with leaves more loosely grouped.

GROWING IN SMALL SPACES

If your area gets hard freezes in winter, you will find it best to grow sweet marjoram in a container so it can be overwintered indoors. Water occasionally throughout the winter. Sweet marjoram can be short-lived if grown indoors or in greenhouses due to its susceptibility to root and stem diseases.

HARVESTING

Sweet marjoram can be harvested fresh anytime during the growing season. With garden shears, trim stems down to about 6 inches (15.2 cm). The leaves dry quickly and retain their flavor well if kept in an airtight container.

DID YOU KNOW?

Medieval herbalists would prescribe sweet marjoram for those "who are given to over-much sighing."

The flowers of this herb give it the traditional name of "knot marjoram." The flower buds that appear in summer form tight green clusters that resembled, to our ancestors, the intricately woven knots sometimes used in place of buttons to secure clothes.

In the "language of flowers," sweet marjoram symbolizes "blushes" and "maidenly innocence."

IN THE GARDEN

THYME

Thyme is a must-have herb for any size herb garden. Of all the herbs you'll grow for flavor, none is more lovely in the garden and delightful in the kitchen than thyme. It comes in a variety of colors and flavors.

THE BASICS

Thyme (*Thymus vulgaris*) is a low-growing perennial hardy to Zone 6. The tiny oval leaves grow thickly on the 8- to 10-inch (20.3 to 25.4 cm) stems. It blooms in early summer, creating a source of nectar that is the delight of bees everywhere. A native of the mountainous regions of Europe, thyme will grow in areas with full sun or part shade.

COMMON VARIETIES

All culinary thymes are small perennial shrubs with spikes of pink, purple, or white flowers. 'Silver' thyme has silver-edged, gray-green leaves that are attractive in hanging baskets. 'Golden' thyme provides color contrast in the garden. Lemon thyme (*Thymus* x *citriodorus*) is a spreading thyme with tiny egg-shaped leaves. Caraway thyme

(*Thymus herba-barona*) has more of a spicy flavor than most thymes. It is a good choice for gardeners in regions with high humidity.

CARE AND FEEDING

Thyme is happiest growing in spots with lots of sunshine and well-drained, almost gravelly, soil. When setting it out in the garden, plant thyme 12 to 18 inches (30.5 to 45.7 cm) apart near the front of your garden bed. Thyme needs regular watering during the first year but can withstand arid conditions once established.

Thyme is a modest herb that spreads slowly. Prune in spring and fall by clipping the stems down to about 6 inches (15.2 cm) high. This will maintain the plant's health as it reduces the amount of less-productive, old wood.

After about three years, rejuvenate your thyme by dividing it in the fall. Dig up the main clump and with a sharp knife separate the root mass into two or three sections. Remove any dead or badly damaged sections. Replant the new sections and water to settle the roots.

In an ornament garden, combine a planting of thyme with perennial bulbs, such as lilies and daffodils. The stalks will push through the thyme in early spring, flower, and die back before the thyme starts to take off in late spring. Then throughout the growing year, you'll have a ground cover while the bulbs are lying dormant.

GROWING IN SMALL SPACES

All varieties of thyme grow well in containers. Their tiny leaves contrast nicely with other herbs such as basil, parsley, and onion chives. Allow thyme to cascade over the side for a pleasing visual effect.

HARVESTING

Clip fresh thyme anytime during the growing season. Immerse the stems in water to remove debris. Spin or pat dry and place in a large bowl or brown paper bag to dry. Remove the dried leaves from the stems by pinching the tip and moving your fingers down the stems.

DID YOU KNOW?

The dried flowers of thyme were once used to add scent to linens and preserve them from insects.

Oil of thyme is used in toothpastes, mouthwashes, and cough syrups for its antiseptic, antioxidant, and antifungal properties.

In the days of chivalry, knights would often carry a scarf embroidered by their lady with a bee hovering over a sprig of thyme.

IN THE GARDEN

WINTER SAVORY

If you're looking for a warming herb, you can't go wrong with winter savory. Small and unassuming in the garden, this herb provides a peppery flavor that wakes up the taste buds and blends well with a wide range of foods.

THE BASICS

Winter savory (*Satureja montana*) is a low-growing perennial herb hardy to Zone 6. Its 1-inch (2.5 cm)-long green leaves grow on woody branches that spread about 2 feet (61 cm) wide. It grows best with regular watering but can withstand an occasional drought. Spikes of small, white to pink flowers (A) appear in early summer and are much enjoyed by passing bees. It is native to the mountainous regions of Europe.

COMMON VARIETIES

Winter savory has a close relative known as—you guessed it—summer savory (*Satureja hortensis*) (B). This is a tender annual that grows about twice as tall and half as dense as winter savory but has a similar flavor. It grows best in cooler climates and is likely to die out during hot summers. When purchasing, check the botanical name on the pot tag to make sure you get the one you want.

In the western United States, you may also come across a third member of the savory family: yerba buena (*Satureja douglasii*). It is much smaller than winter or summer savory, growing only about 4 inches (10 cm) high. It is also much stronger in flavor and should be used sparingly in foods.

CARE AND FEEDING

Winter savory is a short-lived, low-growing shrub perennial lasting two to three years. Plant this herb where it can receive at least half a day of full sun in well-drained or rocky soil. Soil that is too moist can cause root rot, especially during the winter.

Winter savory can happily grow with your flowering plants. For example, you can plant winter savory at the front edge of a bed with shrub roses growing behind it. Because of its dense growth, winter savory can also be trimmed and used as a low hedge between sections of your garden, as one would when creating a formal knot garden.

Winter savory propagates best by cuttings or layering. In the spring, look for side branches that have touched the ground and rooted during the winter. These can be clipped and removed from the parent plant to grow elsewhere or extend your bed of winter savory. Lightly trim as needed to maintain a pleasing shape and encourage new growth.

GROWING IN SMALL SPACES

Winter savory can easily be trimmed to fit in a limited space garden. It will also grow nicely in containers or hanging baskets.

HARVESTING

Clip and use fresh winter savory anytime, winter or summer. To dry winter savory, harvest before it flowers in early summer.

DID YOU KNOW?

Some people call winter savory "the bean herb" for its reputed ability to curb the flatulence associated with beans.

In Medieval times, winter savory was considered a sexual appetite suppressant because of its association with the cooler, less passionate months.

Before black pepper was commonly available in the Western world, winter savory was used to provide the "heat" in foods. Modern cooks should remember this when using it.

HARVESTING AND PRESERVING HERBS

Harvesting herbs is the delicious payoff for all the hard work of planting, watering, and weeding an herb garden. There's nothing quite like having your arms full of homegrown herbs fresh from your garden. So it's really no surprise that anytime herb enthusiasts get together there are questions about harvesting.

HOW SOON AFTER PLANTING CAN I BEGIN HARVESTING?

A woman holding a just-purchased herb in a 4-inch (10 cm) pot once asked how soon she could harvest from this plant. She confessed that it smelled so delicious she wanted to clip some that very evening. While her enthusiasm was understandable, the plant was very young and any immediate harvest, however small, would weaken the plant.

Once you plant an herb, it takes about a week to recover from the shock and resume normal growth. During that time, roots are reestablished so that water and soil nutrients can be absorbed. Once that is complete, new growth will appear. Be patient and wait until that young herb has at least doubled in volume before clipping any for immediate use.

HOW CAN I MAKE SURE MY HERBS TASTE THEIR BEST?

All herbs contain high amounts of essential oils tucked away in their leaves, stems, and flowers. Essential oils are the natural substances in herbs that provide the flavor, fragrance, and medicinal potency we value. These oils are concentrated in tiny capsules on the surface.

Imagine for a moment you are looking at a fresh herb leaf through a microscope. On the surface, you will see tiny pockets of essential oils encased in a waxy film. These oils are highly volatile, meaning they will evaporate quickly if exposed to the air, leaving little or no residue. Whenever you brush against or spray water on a fresh leaf, you disturb that waxy film and release the essential oils underneath.

How does that effect harvesting herbs for long-term storage? Well, the goal now becomes preserving as much of those oils as possible. This is why you should never use high temperatures when drying herbs because the heat will drive off the oils. This is also why it is best to preserve leaves and seeds in whole form. The less you do to break up those wax-covered pockets, the more flavor and aroma you will have when you finally use it.

I'VE HEARD IT'S BEST TO CUT HERBS IN THE MORNING. IS THAT TRUE?

The most common advice is to harvest "in the morning before 10 a.m." I've never been happy with that answer. Is the morning really better?

A big factor in the time-of-day question is the effect of daytime temperatures on the concentration of essential oils in the herb leaves. Ideally, you want to harvest when they are at their peak. Commercial harvesting is generally done early in the morning or late in the day. They want the harvested material to be as cool as possible when clipped to avoid driving out the volatile essential oils before the drying process is complete. So take a tip from the professionals—when harvesting large amounts, do it when the air is cool in the morning or evening.

HOW SHOULD I CLIP MY HERBS?

Before starting to harvest, make sure your plants are well watered and not stressed. Healthy, happy herbs yield the best flavor. Then gather your gloves and harvesting equipment. Use sharp clippers so you don't mangle the stems. Have something to carry the clipped herbs: a bucket, a large basket, or grocery bags will do the trick.

Perennial herbs such as oregano, sage, and thyme (A) are the simplest to harvest. Cut about one-third to one-half of the plant's height anytime during the growing season. For herbs such as chervil, parsley, and chives (B) that have leaves growing from a central cluster, clip about one-fourth of the leaves, making the cut 1 or 2 inches (2.5 to 5 cm) above the soil line. The flavor of herb leaves varies depending on the age of the leaf. Herb leaves that have overwintered are definitely past their "sell by" date. Just-budded leaves of early spring are weak in flavor compared to leaves that have had time to mature. You want to harvest leaves that are mature, but not from last year's growth.

Basil, chervil, and other annual herbs grown for their leaves can also be harvested periodically from late spring through summer. Wait until they have reached at least half of their final height before making your first cut. Many annuals actually benefit from periodic harvesting. Removing the top part of the stem stimulates formation of new branches and a bushier plant. Clipping the tops also delays them going to seed and encourages your herbs to focus on growing leaves.

WHAT ABOUT HARVESTING SEEDS AND FLOWERS?

Gathering dill, coriander, and other seeds requires more careful timing. Watch for the seeds to plump and turn brown. Clip the heads immediately or you'll lose your harvest to hungry birds or high winds. Clip the umbrella-like seed heads and place them upside down in a brown paper bag. Allow the seeds to ripen for about a week before removing them from the seed head and storing in an airtight jar.

Harvest edible herb flowers such as onion chives and pot marigold when the flowers have just opened. The heads will be firm and at maximum flavor. Handle them gently to minimize damage.

For all your herbs, harvest only parts that are in good condition. Leaves, seeds, or flowers that are damaged or wilted won't improve after they're clipped.

WHAT'S THE BEST WAY TO DRY HERBS?

You've probably seen photos of herbs hanging upside down in bunches to dry (D). It looks pretty, but that's not how I would recommend preserving herbs for cooking. Instead, lay the stalks in a single layer on an absorbent towel placed on a flat surface (E). Allow them to air-dry for at least six to eight days, more for thick-leaved herbs such as sage and rosemary. Once the leaves become dry and crackly, store them in an airtight container away from light.

During the drying process, it's important to prevent mold from taking hold. Each day during the drying, fluff the herb stalks to expose new parts to the air. If you live in a humid area, consider using a small fan to prevent decay. In hot weather, take advantage of the relatively high temperatures in your garage and the trunk of your car for "express drying."

Both the oven and the microwave will speed the drying of herbs. The problem is that they are likely to drive out some of the essential oils in the process. The lowest setting on many conventional ovens is 200°F (93°C). Essential oils will begin evaporating somewhere around 140°F (60°C), leaving you with less flavorful dried herbs. Microwaves heat foods unevenly and can only safely dry about a handful of herbs at a time. But even then, you will find some portions of the herbs drying out faster than others. As far as I'm concerned, laying herbs out to dry naturally works just fine without any significant loss of essential oils.

CAN I FREEZE MY HERBS?

Some herbs such as basil and parsley can be frozen in whole leaf form to maximize flavor preservation. Remove the just-harvested leaves from the stems and rinse them well (F). Eliminate excess moisture by using a terry cloth towel to pat them dry or spinning the leaves in a salad spinner. Lay the leaves flat, in a single layer on a tray, and place in the freezer. The leaves are so thin they will freeze in an hour or so. Remove the tray from the freezer, gather the frozen leaves into an airtight plastic bag or container, and return them to the freezer. Leaves can be later removed and defrosted as needed.

Freezing onion chives is just as easy. Rinse and pat dry the whole leaves. With kitchen scissors, snip the chive leaves into small sections and scatter them on a baking tray. Place the tray in the freezer for an hour. Remove from the freezer, pour the chives into an airtight plastic bag or container, and return them to the freezer.

If you plan to use your herbs in a finely chopped form for such things as pesto, sauces, or soups, you can puree and freeze them. Take the fresh leaves of basil, cilantro, or other herbs and place them in a food processor. Add a small amount of water and process the leaves until finely chopped into a thick liquid form. Pour the pureed leaves into an ice cube tray and freeze. Later remove the frozen cubes of herbs from the tray and store in a freezer bag. Now you have small frozen portions of your herb ready to use throughout the year.

HARVESTING HINTS

Clip during the cooler part of the day—morning or evening, your choice.

Harvest when the leaves are healthy and have good flavor.

Avoid harvesting when the plants are stressed from drought or heat.

Enjoy the results.

SECTION 2
IN THE KITCHEN

The days of thinking of fresh herbs as a garnish or breath freshener are long gone. Today, the culinary world is benefitting from the many uses of fresh herbs inspired by globalization. Routinely adding fresh herbs—especially those that you have grown yourself—to your culinary repertoire is not only en vogue but is also a simple way to enhance your cooking in a healthy, economical, and deliciously creative way.

This section of the book is a mini cooking school using fresh herbs as the common thread. Although there are classic herb dishes (for example, you cannot have an herb book without a recipe for salsa verde or pesto), each one has a modern twist.

Each chapter begins with a discussion of which flavors and foods pair well with that particular herb and how to prepare that herb for use in your kitchen. A collection of recipes using that herb follows. The recipes use a range of foods and use the herb at various stages in the cooking process. And many of the recipes overall are interchangeable and can serve as the basis for your own creations.

Because herbs are so versatile, you will be learning traditional cooking techniques and methods, including sautéing, poaching, steaming, grilling, baking, roasting pan frying, deep-frying, confit, stir-frying, steaming en papillote, soufflé, roulade (rolling), and farce (stuffing), at the same time you are learning about herbs.

COOKING WITH HERBS

When I give cooking classes, I often make analogies to everyday life situations and common phrases to make things easier to remember. With respect to fresh herbs I have this tidbit: green is the new black—in culinary terms, of course.

In both my professional and my personal life, I use herbs with abandon. They create a fuller flavor in a light, delicate way. Fresh herbs breathe life into a dish and they mark it with evidence of your careful attention. Flowering herbs are even more of a delight. When my rosemary, chive, thyme, and coriander plants are flowering, I use both the leaves and the flowers as much as I can.

When I teach, I tell students that cooking is a combination of three factors: (1) learning a few basic skills; (2) purchasing seasonal, local foods, which are naturally the most flavorful; and (3) gaining knowledge of the food itself. My mantra is: "know your ingredients; respect their character."

Herbs are a great example. If you know what the herb tastes like, how best to use it, and which flavors and foods it pairs well with, the possibilities of creating beautiful, tasty dishes are limitless. The rest of this book will give you this knowledge and provide you with recipes demonstrating each herb's range of culinary possibilities.

USING FRESH HERBS

Generally speaking, herbs can be used in both sweet and savory preparations. On the savory side, herbs enhance stews, braises, sautés, soups, court-bouillon for poaching, fumets, and steaming liquid. They can serve as a primary ingredient for salads, tartares, and chilled soups.

As you will see throughout these recipes, fresh herbs can be used in a variety of ways to enhance the flavor of a meat protein. Before cooking, herbs can be used in a brine, a marinade, or a rub. During the cooking process, herbs can be used to flavor a whole fish, poultry, or game as well as filets and vegetarian options, such as squash or eggplant. An herb crust can add a beautiful contrast of green color and texture to meats such as beef tenderloin, lamb chops, or fish and also act as a moistening and flavoring agent.

Herbs can add a boost of flavor at the end of the cooking process. Minced herbs can be added to butter to create a compound butter (A) for a finishing touch to a perfectly cooked steak or baked fish. Herbs added to jus, butter, or stock can create a colorful and tasty sauce or emulsion.

Beyond main dishes, fresh herbs add zing to salad dressings and other condiments such as mayonnaise, aioli, mustard, and hollandaise. Herbs can be added to an olive tapenade.

Pesto and gremolata (an herb, garlic, and lemon zest garnish traditionally used in osso buco) have many uses and bring an immediate freshness and color to uniform purées, such as those made from potatoes, broccoli, sweet potatoes, artichokes, or fennel. They add flavor and color to pizza dough, breads, raw and cooked vegetables, gnocchi, and pasta. Minced rosemary or thyme can be added to snacks items, such as chips, crackers, french fries, spiced or sweetened roasted nuts, and baked granola.

Herbs can be added to preserves such as jams and gelées (both sweet and savory). They can turn oils, vinegars, salts, sugars, and honeys into flavorful treats. Picture minted-sugar for strawberries (or even sugared whole mint leaves) and walnuts or oranges with rosemary-infused honey, for example. Fresh goat cheese, such as Sainte Maure or crottin de chèvre, and kitchen cheeses, such as burrata, cream cheese, or ricotta, are delicious when marinated or wrapped in fresh herbs. (However, if you use fresh herbs to flavor oils, such oils should be kept in the refrigerator because oils encourage the growth of the botulism bacteria.)

On the sweet side, herbs can infuse flavor to custards, pastry creams, panna cotta, flan, and frozen desserts such as sorbet and ice cream. Herbs can also be added to various cakes, breads, and soufflés and served with fresh, grilled, or poached fruit.

Fresh herbs can be used for a hot infusion or iced for an herbal iced tea. A fresh herb sprig adds zing and visual interest to cocktails and nonalcoholic beverages. Fresh herb leaves can be frozen in ice cubes and added to your beverage for a burst of color (B).

Beyond these culinary applications, herbs are part of a recommended varied diet and have been used for medicinal purposes throughout the ages. For example, basil has been reported to ease colds and flus. Mint is said to ease indigestion. And the simple addition of herbs is a low-calorie way to boost of flavor of even the most ordinary meal (3½ ounces [100 g] of basil is a mere 23 calories, and a handful of basil leaves is only 1 ounce [28 g]).

B

GRASSY AND WOODY HERBS

Although most herbs belong to the mint or carrot family (the shape of the leaf is a giveaway as to which one), I break herbs down into two categories based upon their flavor and texture: grassy or woody. These are not technical terms, but practical classifications that are easy to remember.

Grassy herbs infuse a burst of fresh, grassy brightness to a dish with notes of citrus, anise, and mint (C). They include basil, chives, chervil, dill, parsley, cilantro, mint, tarragon, and savory. Grassy herbs can be used as primary contributors in a dish because of their fresh, delicate flavor. Chervil and parsley are the most used because they are light and neutral in flavor. Basil, chives, mint, and cilantro can also be used in a primary way in some soups, salads, and egg preparations.

Basil, tarragon, mint, and savory are grassy herbs with a spike of a woody personality (D). The stems generally are not eaten (unless the leaves are smaller and tender, and then so too are the stems). These grassy herbs have stronger notes and are therefore used with a lighter hand. For example, in a fines herbes combination, which classically calls for an equal amount of tarragon, parsley, chives, and chervil, some cooks recommend using less tarragon. Similarly, too much basil in a dish can result in an overly minty or anise taste.

Woody herbs have stronger personalities than grassy herbs. The leaves and stems are tougher and tend to be a little pungent. Woody herbs include sage, thyme, bay laurel, rosemary, lemongrass, and marjoram. The stems of woody herbs are not eaten. They are almost never used as a primary ingredient. If you use too much of a woody herb, the resulting dish can be medicinal tasting.

Whether the herb is grassy or woody suggests a general proper pairing of flavors and preparations. For example, a woody herb tends to be well suited for warm flavors prevalent in the fall and winter seasons (apples, pears, mushrooms, winter squashes, chestnuts, and simmered beans) and food preparations used more in the colder months such as stews, braises, and ragouts. Woody flavors are best with oily, more substantial fish, red meats, game, pork, and poultry.

Conversely, grassy herbs generally tend to be well suited for cooler flavors and raw or gentle preparations typical of the spring and summer months (salads, tartares, chilled soups, egg preparations, light fish, and poultry) and are best with poaching, steaming, and grilling. Grassy herbs taste best with hydrating fruits (such as tomatoes, stone fruits, berries, melons, cucumbers, and summer squash), young green spring vegetables, and seafood, including delicate fish.

HOW HERBS RELEASE THEIR FLAVOR

According to Harold McGee, author of *On Food and Cooking* and an authority on the properties of foods and their chemical makeups, the flavor in herbs comes from volatile essential oils, which easily escape from the herb through heat or cutting or crushing the leaves.

Whether an herb is grassy or woody indicates the optimal time to use it in the cooking process. The oils in woody herbs are less volatile than the oils in grassy herbs. Therefore, woody herbs need to be added early in the cooking process to release their flavor into the food. (This is why they are often used in stews, braises, sautés, steams, roasts, and smoking.) In contrast, the flavor of the more volatile grassy herbs will be lost or modified by even brief cooking (and the sprigs will be limp and lifeless looking). Grassy herbs are therefore generally added to a dish at the end of the cooking process or before serving.

In addition to the use of heat, how herbs are cut affects the flavor. For example, the more you cut the leaves, the more rapidly the flavor is released. Finely minced herbs diffuse a delicate flavor because much of the flavor has escaped. For this reason, if I am mincing an herb, such as cilantro or parsley, for a last-minute addition, I mince the herb two-thirds of the way ("par-cut") and then further chop the leaves to the exact size I want just before serving to preserve the fresh factor.

Adding whole leaves to a dish will impart a bigger fresh flavor because it is literally the diner's teeth that cuts the leaves by chewing, releasing the herb flavor.

If you crush the herbs with a mortar and pestle, less air is incorporated into the herb than when you use a food processor and the herb flavor stays more intact. On the other hand, mincing herbs in a food processor with oil seems to captures the herb's rapid release of flavor.

TASTE, TEXTURE, AND APPEARANCE

When using herbs, it is up to you, the cook, to decide how much of a role you want the herb to play. Also, what do you want the texture of the dish to feel like? What appearance do you want the dish to have? Answers to these questions will dictate how and how much of the herb to use.

Do you want the herb to enhance the flavor of a dish or change the flavor profile? Let's use Italian parsley as an example. Whole parsley leaves (and tender stems) can be used in an herb salad on equal footing with other greens and herbs. In this example, Italian parsley is a component responsible for the overall flavor profile of the salad. Taking a bite of a salad with whole parsley stems and leaves imparts a substantial grassy, fresh taste in each bite. Using a smaller quantity of whole parsley stems and leaves will impart the same substantial grassy flavor but to a lesser degree and allow other components of the salad to dominate. On the opposite end of the spectrum, use just a few whole leaves for a light embellishment with purpose.

If you want to merely boost or brighten the salad without changing its flavor or character, add chopped or finely minced parsley leaves to impart a grassy note consistently throughout.

When you use whole herb leaves, the leaves themselves become a focal point. In turn, minced, shredded, or chopped leaves are not given visual priority but can add a splash of color (it can be a contrasting color or the same) in varying degrees, depending upon how much is added. The mere

shape of the herb itself can be used to a cook's advantage. Chives can be used for their flexible length, and the fibrous stem of lemongrass can be used as a skewer.

PREPARING HERBS

Wash herbs and dry them well before you cut or use them (E). Laying the herbs in between paper towels and gently pressing down helps remove the moisture from the herbs (F).

To cut herbs, use a very sharp chef's knife. A dull blade will bruise the leaves rather than cut them cleanly; this will discolor the leaves, rendering them an unappealing and

flavorless brown or black. When making pesto, the preferred method is to use a mortar and pestle to crush the leaves. For basil and mint, I pluck the leaves from the stems by hand.

Woody herbs and grassy herbs, such as tarragon and savory, are on stems, which you can "strip" in order to remove the leaves or needles. Run your thumb and pointer finger along the stem in the opposite way in which the leaves grow and as you do, pull the leaves or needles from the stem.

FRESH VERSUS DRIED HERBS

Whether the herbs are grassy or woody determines whether they are good candidates for drying. Herbs are mostly water. Grassy herbs lose their flavor when dried because their strength lies in their fresh taste. When you take away the moisture, the "fresh, grassy" factor is gone and you are left with essentially hay. Dried basil and tarragon also lose their "fresh" appeal in my opinion. On the other hand, woody herbs dry well.

Fresh and dried herbs cannot be used interchangeably. Woody herbs take on a stronger flavor when they dry (they are more concentrated because there is no moisture in the product to dilute its properties). The degree of increased concentration varies. Bay is the exception—fresh bay leaves are stronger then dried ones.

Lastly, whether herbs are fresh or dried makes a difference as to when you add the herbs in your cooking. Dried herbs (usually woody herbs) are never added at the end of the cooking, as fresh herb are. It is also recommended that dried herbs be cooked for at least 30 minutes to eliminate any microorganisms that may be present.

USING THIS SECTION

Following are a few ingredient and equipment notes before you get started.

- All the recipes in this book use fresh herbs.

- You will notice that many recipes call for the use of gros sel de Guérande. This is a large salt, hand-combed from the salt beds in Guérande, France. It has a high mineral content, and I love its flavor. It is available on the Internet and in many specialty stores. If you cannot find it, then use quality sea salt. Do not substitute table salt or kosher salt as it is much smaller than sea salt and an equal substitution will make your dish salty.

- Some of the recipes specify "bottled water" because the tap water in some areas has a chorine or metallic taste. If the tap water in your area tastes good, then bottled water is not necessary.

- When it comes to mincing herbs, I find a mini food processor to be preferable because the regular size is too large. However, you can always chop by hand with a chef's knife, so special equipment is not necessary in any event.

GENERAL COOKING TIPS

Cooking is about using your senses. Look at the appearance of the food. Smell it. Taste it. Salt early and readjust the seasoning and consistency at the end of the cooking process.

Review the entire recipe before you begin. Remember that recipe measurements of quantity and time (1 cup [235 ml] stock, ½ teaspoon salt, 10 minutes) are guidelines that may vary according to your circumstances. Variables can include the weather, oven accuracy, the flavor and age of the ingredients, a flame's height, the sodium content of the stock used, and even household distractions.

Don't be afraid to adjust. If a purée looks too thick, for example—if it has the consistency of a dip rather than a creamy purée—add more liquid even if you already added the quantity the recipe called for.

Lastly, I have tried to provide you with cooking times where applicable, but remember that the determination of when a dish is done is not dictated by a clock. Rather, it is the appearance, feel, and temperature of the food that is relevant. If your french fries are not golden brown and crispy, then they are not done regardless of what the timer says.

Zucchini and Basil Soufflé with Basil Cream, page 56

IN THE KITCHEN

BASIL

Sweet basil, once used by the ancient Greeks, is prevalent in Mediterranean foods and goes well with foods used in Provençal and Italian cooking: tomatoes, olives, olive oil, lamb, summer squash, eggplant, onions, garlic, lemon, and zucchini blossoms. This grassy herb, with flavors of mint, anise, tarragon, and pepper, is the dominant flavor in pesto Genovese from Genoa and pestou from Provence. (See 140 for a primer on pesto.) Basil is perfect in a simple tomato tartare.

PAIRINGS

Basil goes well with hard Italian cheeses (such as Parmesan), French goat cheese (chèvre and crottin), and kitchen cheeses (such as mozzarella, burrata, ricotta, and even cream cheese). And it is a nice complement to pine nuts, almonds, walnuts, and pistachios.

It also pairs nicely with a range of fish (salmon, tuna, loup de mer, daurade, halibut, and snapper), but it is best with moderately oily fish. (I find it a little strong for delicate fish such as sole.) It is wonderful with other seafood as well, including crab, shrimp, scallops, lobster, mussels, clams, and calamari, and it is excellent in seafood tartares and ceviches. The whole leaves add a fresh finishing touch to seafood stews or soups. It also goes well with tofu, beef, and poultry.

Basil is wonderful with hydrating fruits such as raspberries, blueberries, blackberries, strawberries, and melons, particularly watermelon and cantaloupe, and summer stone fruit such as apricots, nectarines, and peaches. Fresh basil leaves balance the sweetness of grilled or pan-fried fruit with a simple syrup.

Basil goes well with dairy products such as buttermilk, cream, crème fraîche, and sour cream as well as eggs. Chopped or shredded leaves greatly enhance pasta, rice, and couscous, and basil is often added to condiments such as mayonnaise.

The herb can be used in conjunction with other greens and grassy herbs, including cilantro, parsley, chives, chervil, mint, and lemon verbena. It is used often as a substitute for cilantro because it is less pungent. My favorite varieties of basil are 'Genovese' and 'Purple Ruffles', which has leaves that are exactly that— purple and ruffled.

Thai basil is sometimes used in place of sweet basil. It has more of a peppery-anise taste than sweet basil. It is hugely prevalent in Asian cuisine, and it is becoming more popular in cuisines in Europe and the United States. Thai basil pairs well with sweet and citrusy foods, including winter squash (such as sugar pumpkin and kabocha) and tropical fruits like pineapple, coconut, mango, and papaya. Thai basil complements vanilla, ginger, curry, lemongrass, and citrus flavors (orange, lemon, lime, and yuzu). It is often added whole with other fresh herbs in Vietnamese dishes, including pho.

HOW TO USE
Basil leaves can be used whole, by simply plucking them off of the stems. The leaves can be torn or coarsely (rough) chopped or cut into a chiffonade (shredded) in various widths.

To chiffonade basil, gather the leaves in a uniform pile and roll (A). Use a sharp knife to make parallel cuts along the length of the rolled leaves (B). For a more delicate texture and flavor, make the cuts closer together to make a fine chiffonade (C). A fine chiffonade is the best way to release the basil flavor in a marinade or dressing. Remember to keep herb-infused oils in the refrigerator to avoid the growth of bacteria.

For optimal flavor in salads and raw preparations, add whole basil leaves to the dish. When adding whole leaves to a salad or raw preparation, I prefer to use the smaller or moderate-size leaves, as large leaves can become a little too anise-tasting. For a less uniform presentation, you can tear or roughly chop the leaves.

BASIL WRAPS

This easy, summery recipe combines whole basil leaves with the familiar flavors of the Mediterranean. Leaving the leaves whole gives each wrap a maximum fresh basil taste. The wraps can be a snack, a canapé, or served with soup.

2 tablespoons (28 ml) quality balsamic vinegar or balsamic glaze or crema

6 tablespoons (90 ml) quality fruity olive oil

Gros sel de Guérande or sea salt, as needed

8 slices of prosciutto

8 large basil leaves, plus more for garnish

4 handfuls of green salad-herb mixture (such as mesclun, red and green tango, arugula, tatsoi, mizuna, baby chard, beet greens, mint, and basil leaves)

12 toothpicks

Place the balsamic vinegar in a bowl. Whisk in the olive oil. Add a pinch of salt. Set aside.

Lay the prosciutto slices flat on a cutting board. Place 1 large basil leaf on top of each prosciutto slice. Add some salad on top of each basil leaf (don't make it too big). Roll the prosciutto from one end to the other, enveloping the basil and salad inside; secure with a toothpick. Garnish with a basil leaf and serve immediately.

YIELD: 4 SERVINGS

NOTE

Balsamic glaze or crema is balsamic vinegar that has been thickened by reduction and sweetened with sugar. You can make your own version at home by placing ¾ cup (175 ml) balsamic vinegar and about ½ cup (115 g) packed brown sugar in a saucepan. Simmer, reducing the liquid until you achieve a syrupy consistency. Remember that the liquid will thicken more as it cools.

KABOCHA AND COCONUT SOUP WITH THAI BASIL LEAVES

Thai basil pairs well with tropical flavors and nicely balances sweet ingredients (here, kabocha squash). Adding fresh, whole Thai basil leaves to the soup lends a fresh twist on a hearty winter soup. It is also a great way to use leftover chicken or Thanksgiving turkey.

1 kabocha squash

Olive oil, as needed

Kosher salt, as needed

1 tablespoon (14 g) unsalted butter

1 clove of garlic, minced

2 tablespoons (20 g) minced shallot

½ teaspoon finely grated ginger

About 2¼ cups (535 ml) chicken stock

Bouquet garni (1 bay leaf and Italian parsley, tied with kitchen twine)

½ cup (120 ml) unsweetened coconut milk

½ teaspoon lemon zest

Freshly ground black pepper, as needed

Thai basil leaves, as needed

Shredded cooked chicken or turkey (optional)

Preheat the oven to 375°F (190°C, or gas mark 5).

Cut the squash in half and remove the seeds. Rub the flesh with olive oil and sprinkle with kosher salt. Place face down in a baking dish or a sheet pan lined with parchment paper. Roast the squash until the flesh is tender and the skin can easily be peeled from the flesh (don't overcook or it will be dry). Set aside. When the squash is cool enough to handle, peel the skin and discard. Chop and weigh the squash. You need 13 ounces (365 g).

Place a saucepan over medium heat and add the butter. When the butter is melted, add the shallots and sauté until translucent. Add the ginger and the squash and toss to coat with the butter. Add the stock and bouquet garni and stir to combine. Bring to a boil. Reduce the heat and simmer for about 20 minutes. Discard the bouquet garni.

Use an immersion blender (or a food processor) to purée until very smooth. Strain through a sieve into a clean pot. Add the coconut milk, lemon zest, and chicken and heat through. Adjust the seasoning with salt and pepper. Adjust the consistency (the soup should be the consistency of cold cream). If the soup is too thick, but the flavor profile is good, add a little water. If the soup needs a flavor boost, add a little more stock. If the soup is too thin, continue to simmer until it thickens.

Add the Thai basil leaves to each soup bowl before serving.

YIELD: 2 TO 4 SERVINGS

HEIRLOOM TOMATO AND PEACH SUMMER SALAD

Combining fresh basil leaves with juicy tomatoes and lush peaches, this salad is a beautiful way to begin a summer meal. The dressing can be made in advance. The salad can be served with a side of burrata cheese. Serve with crusty French bread.

2 ripe yellow peaches	3 tablespoons (45 ml) quality olive oil
2 heirloom tomatoes	1 teaspoon minced shallot
1 tablespoon (15 ml) Champagne vinegar	Gros sel de Guérande or sea salt, as needed
1 teaspoon fresh orange juice	Tender basil leaves

Wash and dry the peaches. Cut in half, remove the pits, and slice each half into quarters. Core the tomatoes. Slice the tomatoes the same size as the peaches. Place the tomatoes and peaches in a bowl.

Combine the vinegar and orange juice in a bowl. Whisk in the olive oil. Add the shallot and salt. Whisk to blend.

Pour half of the dressing over the salad. Use your hands to gently coat the peaches and tomatoes in the dressing. Add more dressing as needed. Divide the salad equally on chilled plates. Add the basil leaves in a beautiful way.

YIELD: 4 SERVINGS

ZUCCHINI AND BASIL SOUFFLÉ WITH BASIL CREAM

Recipe photo appears on page 48

I wrote this recipe after a stay in the south of France, where basil and zucchini are in abundance. The basil cream is a demonstration of imparting a dessert-style cream with a hint of basil. You can make the cream by itself. Chilled and whipped, it makes fresh fruit a delightful yet light dessert.

2 tablespoons (28 g) unsalted butter, plus more for the pan

1 tablespoon (13 g) sugar, plus more for sprinkling

1½ cups (180 g) finely grated zucchini

1 heaping cup (40 g) roughly chopped basil

¼ teaspoon kosher salt

2 tablespoons (28 ml) olive oil

¾ cup (175 ml) milk

⅛ teaspoon freshly ground black pepper

2 or 3 thyme sprigs, stripped

3 tablespoons (24 g) all-purpose flour

2 egg yolks

3 egg whites

Butter a large soufflé dish. Sprinkle with the sugar, tap off the excess, and set aside.

Place the grated zucchini in a sauté pan over medium-high heat. Cook until most of the moisture has been cooked out. Weigh the zucchini. It should weigh 5 ounces (140 g). Place the zucchini, basil, salt, and olive oil in a food processor. Purée. Set aside.

In a saucepan over high heat, scald the milk, pepper, and thyme. Turn off the heat. Melt the remaining 2 table-spoons (28 g) butter in another saucepan. Once melted, whisk the flour into the melted butter. Continue to cook (and whisk) for about 2 to 3 minutes until the flour taste is gone. Whisk the scalded milk into the roux. Turn off the heat and remove from the stove.

Off of the heat (or you will have scrambled eggs), whisk the egg yolks into the mixture one at a time. Add the zucchini-basil purée. This is the soufflé base. Place in a nonreactive bowl. The base can be made in advance and stored it in an airtight container in the refrigerator for up to 2 days (but let it come to room temperature before you finish the recipe).

Preheat the oven to 400°F (200°C, or gas mark 6).

Using a stand mixer fitted with the whisk attachment or a handheld mixer, beat the egg whites on medium speed. When the whites begin look foamy, add the remaining 1 tablespoon (13 g) sugar. Continue to whisk on medium speed until the eggs begin to hold soft peaks and then turn the speed on high. Continue to whisk on high speed until the whites hold firm peaks. If your whites look a little lumpy instead of "peaky," you overmixed and the whites are breaking down. You can start over with fresh eggs, or add another egg white to the broken whites.

Stir one-third of the egg whites into the zucchini base. Gently fold in the remaining whites in thirds using a spatula.

Spoon the mixture into the prepared soufflé dish. Place on a rimmed baking sheet lined with parchment paper and place in the oven on the middle rack. Immediately turn the oven down to 375°F (190°C, or gas mark 5) and bake for about 25 minutes until the soufflé is puffed, the top is golden brown, and the center is set. Serve immediately.

YIELD: ONE 7-INCH (18 CM) SOUFFLÉ

BASIL CREAM

2 tablespoons (26 g) sugar, divided	Pinch of kosher salt
1 egg yolk	¼ teaspoon lemon zest
1 cup (235 ml) heavy whipping cream	1¼ teaspoons cornstarch
1 heaping cup (40 g) roughly chopped basil leaves	1 teaspoon quality olive oil

Whisk together 1 tablespoon (13 g) of the sugar and the egg yolk in a bowl. Set aside. Place the cream, basil, salt, zest, and remaining 1 tablespoon (13 g) of sugar in a saucepan over high heat. Bring to a scald. Slowly pour half of the scalded cream mixture into the yolk mixture while whisking. Return the entire contents of the bowl back to the saucepan with the cream. Add the cornstarch and continue to whisk (and cook) over medium heat until the cornstarch flavor is gone and the cream has thickened. The cream is done when it coats the back of a wooden spoon.

Strain the cream through a sieve into a nonreactive bowl (discard the cooked basil leaves). Stir in the olive oil. The cream can be served warm or at room temperature. The cream can be stored in the refrigerator for a few days.

The cream can be made in advance or while the soufflé is baking.

YIELD: ¼ CUP (60 ML)

*Autumn Pears Poached with Bay,
page 61*

IN THE KITCHEN

BAY LAUREL

Bay laurel is a woody herb that smells like eucalyptus and the woods combined with a hint of mint. It should be used judiciously in cooking—rarely more than two or three fresh leaves—or the resulting dish will be medicinal tasting.

Bay laurel is one of the more commonly used herbs and prevalent in Mediterranean, French, Turkish, and Moroccan cuisines.

PAIRINGS

Bay laurel, known simply as bay in the kitchen, naturally pairs with warm, hearty foods and protracted preparations, such as braising and roasting. Woody herbs, including lemongrass, marjoram, thyme, and sage, go well with bay, and bay complements a range of meats, including beef, lamb, veal, pork, poultry, game birds, venison, wild boar, duck, and goose.

Bay leaves can also be used for an abbreviated, yet purposeful, infusion of flavor for delicate foods and preparations. Bay laurel goes well with seafood, from oily fish such as salmon and monkfish to more delicate fish such as sea bass and even sole.

Instrumental in the preparation of many sauces, ragouts, and braises, bay adds a sweet, woodsy enhancement to starchy dishes, such as risottos, baked potatoes, paellas, creamy polenta, and couscous. Simmered legumes are not the same without an infusion of bay.

Bay pairs well with alliums (garlic, leeks, shallots, and onions), root vegetables and tubers (carrots, parsnips, sweet potatoes, and Jerusalem artichoke), celery root, beets, cauliflower, kale, and cabbage. It is excellent roasted or baked with apples, eggplant, tomatoes, summer squash, or winter squash. A bay leaf is a wonderful enhancement to fruits like figs, grapes, or berries steamed en papillote and in poaching liquids made with port, red wine, white wine, Champagne, or simple sugar to simmer quince, apples, pears, plums, peaches, nectarines, apricots, cherries, and berries. It goes well with maple and date sugars.

Simmer bay leaves in dairy for an infusion of flavor (used in gratins, bread puddings, or a dauphinoise). A bay leaf can be tied to a soft cheese such as Brie, Camembert, or Neufchâtel and stored for a few days in the refrigerator.

Bay pairs nicely with warm-toned spices, such as allspice, cinnamon, juniper berries, and anise stars. Combine a leaf with spices in a cheesecloth sachet for easy removal. Bay is also good with olive oils, lemon, and vinegar. (Cipollini onions cooked with balsamic vinegar and a bay leaf are delicious.)

HOW TO USE

Bay leaves are not eaten. They are best used at the beginning of the cooking process to draw out their flavor. They can be used alone or combined in a bouquet garni (A) or a sachet with spices to flavor braises, broths, soups, simmers, sauces, or a court-bouillon for steaming or poaching. A bay leaf can be added to the cavity of poultry or fish when roasting or poaching.

Use whole bay leaves to "lard" fish, meat, or vegetables during the cooking process by making incisions in the flesh and inserting a leaf or piece of one (B). You can use the bay leaves on skewers to enhance the flavor of a kabob or use a stripped, water-soaked bay stem as a skewer itself. To bring out the bay flavor of a dish with shorter cooking times, gently sauté the bay leaf in oil or with other ingredients, including spices. Lastly, chop or finely grind the bay leaf, alone or in combination with other herbs, for a rub or marinade or to include in a salt to season food before cooking (C).

Bay leaves pose a choking hazard—particularly in soups and stews, where bay leaves may be hidden—so remove them from the dish before serving. A bay leaf can be left in the presentation when it is obvious to the eater that the herb is not meant to be consumed. Examples are when serving poached fruit in a large communal bowl, serving en papillote where the pouch is opened at the table, or when a bay branch is used as a skewer.

BOUQUET GARNI

Bouquet garni is French for "bouquet of garnishments." A bouquet garni adds flavor to stews, braises, ragouts, court-bouillon, soups, and sauces. There are many variations of what constitutes a bouquet garni. This is a classic combination of herbs; common additions include bacon, leeks, winter savory, and celery tops. This particular bouquet garni is excellent in meat braises such a beef bourguignon, coq au vin, winter stews, and vegetarian soups.

1 bay leaf	3 sprigs of thyme
6 stems of Italian parsley	

Gather the bay, parsley, and thyme and tie together with kitchen string. Use the string to remove the bouquet garni from the dish when cooking is done. Discard.

YIELD: 1 BOUQUET GARNI

GREEN SALT RUB

In this rub, bay laurel is combined with a variety of herbs to create a cure that enhances the flavor of various meats before cooking. This rub is inspired by a "green salt" formula used by one of my culinary professors. I use the rub in many preparations, but the woodsy aroma is particularly well suited to game birds such as duck.

½ cup (120 g) kosher salt	2 tablespoons (12 g) sweet marjoram
2 bay leaves	¼ cup (15 g) Italian parsley leaves
2 tablespoons (5 g) thyme leaves	

Place the salt and herbs in a mini food processor and pulse to combine. Generally use about 2 teaspoons of green salt per 1 pound (455 g) of meat or 1 to 2 teaspoons per poultry leg. Rub on meat and place in a covered container in the refrigerator as the recipe indicates. Rinse the salt off before cooking. Unused salt can be stored in the refrigerator for a week or two in an airtight container.

YIELD: ABOUT ½ CUP (170 G)

AUTUMN PEARS POACHED WITH BAY

Recipe photo appears on page 58

Adding a bay leaf to a poaching liquid is a subtle way to infuse flavor in a variety of items. It is particularly nice with fruit. Poached pears can be a simple or an elegant dessert. For casual gatherings, place the pan of poached pears, with its poaching liquid, on the table and serve directly from the pan. For a more elegant presentation, serve the pear individually, whole or sliced, with some ice cream and chocolate sauce (for a classic poire belle Hélène) or a reduction of the poaching liquid. In the summertime, use cherries, apricots, or plums, but remember that because they are less dense, the poaching time will be less. Poach them just until the fruit is soft, but still holds it shape.

Fresh lemon juice, as needed	2 or 3 bay leaves
4 Bosc or Conference pears or 6 Seckel pears	¼ of a vanilla bean pod, split
1 bottle (750 ml) white wine	1¼ cups (250 g) sugar

Fill a bowl with water and add the lemon juice. Set aside. Use a pairing knife to peel the skin from the pears in a circular motion, as smoothly as possible, leaving the stem intact. Place the peeled pear in the bowl of acidulated water. Repeat for all the pears.

Combine the wine, bay leaves, vanilla, and sugar in a saucepan over medium heat. Once the sugar has dissolved, add the pears. Poach the pears until a knife can easily be inserted into the bottom of the pear, about 20 minutes. Remove the pears with a slotted spoon and set aside.

Reduce the liquid until it becomes thicker. Return the pears to the reduced liquid. Serve the pears as described above.

YIELD: 4 TO 8 SERVINGS

DUCK LEG CONFIT WITH HERB SALAD

Confit is both a method of preservation and a method of cooking. Here, it is both. Duck legs are slowly cooked in rendered duck fat. The legs can be stored for weeks in the refrigerator in some of the fat (or shredded and mixed with some fat for rillettes). I like to make a batch of twelve confit duck legs at a time and freeze them in packs of four so I can take them out of the freezer and add them to a variety of dishes for a quick meal. Bay leaf is used twice in this recipe: first in the green salt rub and then in the rendered fat.

½ cup (170 g) Green Salt Rub (page 60)	1 cinnamon stick
12 duck legs	2 star anise pods
About 5 pounds (2.3 kg) rendered duck fat	2 sprigs of thyme
10 mixed peppercorns (pink, black, and green)	3 bay leaves
6 juniper berries	

Rub 1 to 2 teaspoons of the green salt mixture into each duck leg. Place the salted legs in an airtight container and place in the refrigerator for 1 to 2 nights. Rinse well to remove the seasoning from the duck legs and pat dry with a paper towel.

Preheat the oven to 200°F (93°C).

Place a heavy-bottomed pan over low heat. Add the duck fat to the pan and melt. Turn off the heat. Place the duck legs in a large baking dish or Dutch oven and pour over the melted fat, covering them completely. Add the peppercorns, juniper berries, cinnamon, star anise, thyme, and bay leaves to the duck legs and rendered fat.

Cover the baking dish with a lid or aluminum foil. Place in the oven and simmer the duck legs in the fat overnight (about 8 hours) or until the meat is ready to fall off the bone and the rendered fat is clear.

Carefully remove the baking dish from the oven. Cool to room temperature.

Remove the duck legs from the cooking fat with tongs. Use a mesh colander lined with cheesecloth to strain the fat (the strained fat can be reused two or three times if stored in the refrigerator or freezer). The duck legs can be stored in a little duck fat in the refrigerator (or use a food sealer to seal bags of 2 to 4 legs and freeze).

To serve, place a skillet over medium-high heat. Add a little duck fat to the pan. Once melted, add the duck legs. Cook until the skin is golden brown and slightly crisp, about 5 minutes. Serve with the salad.

YIELD: 12 DUCK LEGS

HERB SALAD

1 tablespoon (15 ml) red wine vinegar or port vinegar

1 teaspoon Dijon mustard

3 tablespoons (45 ml) olive oil

1 teaspoon minced shallot

½ teaspoon gros sel de Guérande or sea salt

¼ cup (15 g) Italian parsley leaves

with stems, trimmed

¼ cup (8 g) chervil with stems, trimmed

¼ cup (24 g) mint leaves

2 tablespoons (8 g) French tarragon leaves

8 onion chives, cut into 4-inch (10 cm) lengths

2 handfuls of mesclun greens

Edible flowers, for garnish

Place the vinegar and mustard in a bowl. Combine. Whisk in the oil. Add the shallots and salt and stir. Combine the herbs and mesclun greens in a large bowl. Lightly dress the salad and garnish with the edible flowers.

YIELD: 4 SERVINGS

Poached Sea Bass with Herb Sauce,
page 66

IN THE KITCHEN
CHERVIL

Chervil is the subtlest of the grassy herbs. It is a smaller, more delicate version of Italian parsley with light green leaves. It offers whispers of citrus, anise, and grass. Chervil is available from spring through autumn.

PAIRINGS

Chervil has been popular in French cuisine for years but is not routinely used outside the country. It is best with delicate foods and flavors, such as fish, crab, lobster, clams, mussels, scallops, poultry, veal, and eggs. The flavor and texture of red meat and pork, unless thinly shaved or cured, can be overwhelming for this delicate herb.

In salads, chervil goes beautifully with soft, leafy greens such as butterhead lettuce, mâche, mesclun, tender spinach leaves, and beet greens. It can add a nice contrast to spicy greens such as wild arugula, watercress, and sorrel.

Chervil adds a delicate touch and color contrast to a variety of vegetables and fruits, including asparagus, avocado, beets, baby carrots, fennel, haricots verts, mushrooms, tomatoes, summer squash, winter squash, and potatoes. It adds a touch of whimsy to tropical fruits such as pineapple, kiwi, mango, coconut, and papaya as well as stone fruits such as cherries, apricots, peaches, plums, and nectarines. It can also be used with berries.

Try pairing chervil with legumes such as lentils and garbanzo, fava, soy, and lima beans. Pine nuts, almonds, walnuts, macadamias, pistachios, hazelnuts, and chestnuts also complement chervil, although the larger nuts should be chopped or crushed.

Chervil does well with mint, basil, cilantro, chives, dill, lavender, lemongrass, lemon verbena, parsley, French tarragon, tender French thyme, and lemon thyme. It is part of the fines herbes combination (with tarragon, chives, and Italian parsley; see page 162) and one-third of the traditional sauce messine (combined with tarragon and parsley). It softens the sweet flavors of maple and honey and adds freshness to mustards, citrus, and olive and nut oils such as pistachio, pecan, and walnut.

When it comes to dairy, chervil goes well with soft, creamy cheeses: fresh goat cheese, triple-crème Brie, and kitchen cheeses such mozzarella, burrata, and ricotta. Chervil is used often in combination with heavy cream, crème fraîche, sour cream, and cream cheese.

HOW TO USE

Add chervil to a dish right before serving to preserve its delicate leaves and stems. Chervil easily wilts on hot food, turning its refined stems into a stringy mess resembling mint dental floss. The only time chervil is cooked is when its tiny leaves are laminated in dough or incorporated into an egg dish, such as a soufflé, quiche, omelet, or scrambled eggs.

Chervil can be used with its stems, trimmed to a length of 1 to 2 inches (2.5 to 5 cm). It can be gathered in a little bunch as a garnish on top of a dish or incorporated into cold dishes such as a green or vegetable salad. Chop the leaves for a subtle infusion of flavor throughout a dish or to use in oils, emulsions, dressings, or sauces.

To chop chervil leaves, gather the chervil stems with your right hand and hold the leafy side of the chervil with your left hand. Use a chef's knife in your right hand to cut off the stems (A). (If you are left-handed, do the reverse.) Discard the stems. Gather the leaves into a ball and hold the tip of the blade with your left hand (to secure the knife). Move the knife left to right and back again to cut the chervil smaller. If leaves stick to the knife blade, wipe the blade and return the leaves to the pile (B). This will only take a few chops as the chervil is small to begin with.

POACHED SEA BASS WITH HERB SAUCE

Recipe photo appears on page 64

Here, chervil is used as a garnish as well as a primary ingredient in the herb sauce. I use Baquetta sea bass for its mild, sweet flavor and lean texture. However, you can use most any white fish, such as cod, sole, or halibut.

FOR COURT-BOUILLON:

4 cups (950 ml) bottled water

2 tablespoons (28 ml) dry white wine

1 tablespoon (14 g) unsalted butter

1 stalk of celery, roughly chopped

½ of a yellow onion

1 carrot, roughly chopped

Strip of lemon peel

Handful of Italian parsley

2 bay leaves

10 black peppercorns

1 teaspoon gros sel de Guérande or sea sal

FOR FISH:

4 fillets (4 to 5 ounces each, or
112 or 140 g) fresh sea bass

Kosher salt, as needed

Freshly ground black pepper, as needed

Chervil with trimmed stems, for garnish

Combine all of the court-bouillon ingredients in a saucepan over medium heat. Simmer for 15 minutes to make court-bouillon. Strain. Discard the solids; reserve the liquid.

Heat the court-bouillon in a saucepan and maintain a temperature between 160° and 170°F (71° and 77°C). Add 1 or 2 fillets to the court-bouillon and cook until the fillets are opaque in color and no longer translucent, about 6 minutes. Remove with a slotted spoon. Repeat the process with the remaining fillets, keeping the cooked ones warm on a covered plate. Serve with the herb sauce and garnish with the chervil.

YIELD: 4 SERVINGS

HERB SAUCE

10 chives

1 cup (30 g) chervil leaves, long stems removed

1 cup (60 g) parsley leaves, thick stems removed

¼ teaspoon kosher salt

2 teaspoons fresh lemon juice

½ cup (120 ml) olive oil

Place the chives, chervil, and parsley in a mini food processor and chop. Add the salt and lemon juice and purée. Add the olive oil in increments until you reach the desired consistency.

YIELD: ⅔ CUP (160 ML)

OYSTERS WITH MIGNONETTE

The word *mignonette* can refer to dainty preparations of meat, matchstick fries, and even a small spice sachet used to flavor stews, but this mignonette is a condiment for raw oysters. Traditionally, mignonette served with oysters contains white pepper, but I replace the white pepper with chervil. You can use red or white wine vinegar instead of Champagne; however, red wine vinegar will stain the shallots. Stronger vinegars, like Xérès or Spanish vinegar, can overwhelm oysters, particularly the smaller ones.

¼ cup (60 ml) Champagne vinegar

Zest of 1 lemon

1 tablespoon (10 g) finely minced shallot

1 tablespoon (2 g) chopped chervil leaves, stems removed

12 fresh oysters

Crushed ice, as needed

Combine the vinegar, zest, shallot, and chervil in a bowl and stir to combine. You can make the mignonette a few hours in advance.

Scrub the oyster shells well in cold water. Place one oyster on a towel on a flat, stable counter surface with the flat side up. Secure the oyster in your left hand for shucking. (You may want to wear an oyster mesh glove for protection.) Using your right hand, carefully insert an oyster knife into the oyster hinge, where the two shells come to a point. Twist the knife until you break the hinge. Slide the knife across the bottom of the top shell. Remove the top shell and discard. Slide the knife along the interior of the bottom shell, separating the oyster from the shell. Leave the oyster in the shell and don't drain.

Place the oyster on a bed of crushed ice to keep cold and repeat with the remaining oysters. Spoon a teaspoon of mignonette over each oyster.

YIELD: 1 DOZEN OYSTERS

ROASTED BEET SALAD WITH FRESH CHERVIL

Chervil is most often paired with delicate fish or poultry. It's not frequently seen with something as hearty as beets. However, the combination of sweet, solid beets with frilly, light chervil is as delicious as the color combination is beautiful. Slice the beets as indicated for visual interest and taste variation. This makes a good side dish for terrines and meat dishes.

---

1 pound (455 g) red, golden, and candy beets

3 teaspoons (15 ml) fresh lemon juice, divided

1½ tablespoons (23 ml) quality

olive oil or pistachio oil

¼ teaspoon gros sel de Guérande or sea salt

Handful of chervil, trimmed, for garnish

Preheat the oven to 400°F (200°C, or gas mark 6). Line a baking sheet with parchment paper.

Cut the beet tops from the bulbs and reserve the tops for another use. Wrap the bulbs in aluminum foil and place on the prepared baking sheet. Roast in the oven until a fork can be easily inserted, about 40 minutes. Remove the beets from the oven. Once the beets are cool enough to handle, peel the skin from the beets. Discard the skins and foil.

When the beets are fully cool, slice the red beets horizontally and place in a bowl. Add 2 teaspoons of the lemon juice (to set the red color) and toss. Cut the golden beets into wedges. Dice the candy beets. Add the beets, remaining 1 teaspoon lemon juice, olive oil, and salt to the bowl. Gently combine. Adjust the seasoning with salt as needed.

Arrange beautifully on a plate with the chervil.

....

YIELD: 6 SERVINGS

HARICOT VERT, MANGO, TOMATO, AND LOBSTER SALAD

The Lorraine region of France is home to a delicious tarragon and chervil cream sauce used on fish (Elizabeth David's beautiful version of a sauce messine is quite well known). The dressing for this lobster salad is a lighter version of that herb combination (without the cream). Haricots verts are also known as French green beans. In Paris, it is popular to use them as a prominent ingredient in a salad combination. Here, the thin beans pair nicely with the cherry tomatoes, greens, and chervil but keep the lobster the focus. This is intended to be a first course, but it will serve two as a main course.

FOR COURT-BOUILLON:

5 cups (1.2 L) bottled water

3 tablespoons (60 g) gros sel de Guérande or (45 g) sea salt

1 tablespoon (15 ml) dry white wine

1 celery stalk, roughly chopped

1 carrot, roughly chopped

½ of an onion, halved

Strip of lemon peel

Handful of Italian parsley

3 bay leaves

FOR DRESSING:

2 teaspoons red wine vinegar

2 teaspoons fresh lime juice

6 tablespoons (90 ml) quality olive oil

2 teaspoons heavy cream

2 tablespoons (20 g) minced shallot

2 tablespoons (8 g) minced tarragon

2 tablespoons (4 g) minced chervil

Gros sel de Guérande or sea salt, as needed

FOR SALAD:

1 large handful of haricots verts, trimmed

2 lobster tails

2 dozen cherry heirloom tomatoes, halved

⅓ cup (58 g) diced mango

2 handfuls of mesclun

Chervil leaves, for garnish

Marigold petals, for garnish

To make the court-bouillon: Combine the water, salt, wine, celery, carrot, onion, lemon, parsley, and bay leaves in a saucepan over medium heat. Simmer for 15 minutes. Strain. Discard the solids; reserve the liquid.

To make the dressing: Place the vinegar and lime juice in a bowl. Whisk in the olive oil and cream. Add the shallot, tarragon, and minced chervil. Mix well. Add salt to taste. Set aside.

To make the salad: Place a saucepan of salted water over medium-high heat and bring to a boil. Add the haricots verts and boil for 2 to 3 minutes until crisp-tender. Drain the haricots verts into a colander and place the colander in an ice bath to stop the cooking. Once the haricots verts are cool, drain. Set aside to dry on a paper towel.

In a saucepan, bring the court-bouillon to a simmer over medium heat. Add the lobster tails and cook until the shells are bright red and the tails are no longer translucent. Use tongs to remove the lobster tails. Set aside. When the lobster tails are cool enough to handle, turn the tails belly-side up and use a knife to cut down the middle of the tail through the meat and the shell. Use kitchen scissors to cut the tail in half.

Place the tomatoes, haricots verts, mango, and mesclun in a bowl. Add the dressing, a little at a time, and toss until the salad is lightly coated. Divide the salad among 4 plates. Add ½ a lobster tail on top of the salad. Spoon a little dressing over the lobster flesh.

Garnish with marigold petals and chervil.

....

YIELD: 4 SERVINGS

Skirt Steak with Chimichurri, page 80

IN THE KITCHEN

CILANTRO

Cilantro and coriander are the same plant. Generally speaking, in the Americas, cilantro refers to the green leaves and coriander to the small round seeds. In Europe, coriander refers to both and if the recipe calls for the seeds, it will indicate that.

Cilantro has a grassy, citrusy smell with a cooling component, giving a vivid brightness to whatever it is added to. It resembles flat parsley, but the leaves are thinner and more rounded. If you are confused as to which is which, smell them: cilantro has a strong citrus smell while parsley smells like grass. Some cooks—including Julia Child herself—have an aversion to cilantro and use basil as a substitute.

PAIRINGS

Cilantro is used worldwide more than any other herb. It is prevalent in Asian, Thai, Vietnamese, Caribbean, Portuguese, Middle Eastern, Persian, Turkish, and Mexican cuisines. It is found in everything from Mexican tacos and Vietnamese soups to Middle Eastern stews, falafels, and Turkish gözleme.

The citrus flavor in cilantro pairs well with a range of fish and seafood, including clams, mussels, crab, shrimp, calamari, octopus, cuttlefish, and lobster. It also goes well with other citrus flavors (such as lime and lemon) and Asian flavors, including curry, fresh ginger, and lemongrass. In addition to seafood, cilantro adds a bright note to heavier proteins, including eggs, pork, beef, poultry, and lamb.

The cooling component of cilantro makes it an ideal companion for spicy foods (peppers, radishes, and chiles) as well as other foods with cooling components such as avocados, tomatoes, cucumbers, and apples. Cilantro complements tropical flavors, including coconut, mango, papaya, and pineapple.

Cilantro is often in the company of asparagus, cabbage, onions, scallions, corn, and mushrooms. It breathes freshness into legumes such as beans, lentils, and garbanzo beans, and it is a great addition to rice dishes, orzo, and couscous. It pairs well with semi-hard and salty cheeses such as feta, ricotta, Cheddar, Havarti, and Mexican cheeses.

Cilantro adds freshness to condiments such as guacamole, chimichurri sauce, salsas, salad dressings, and yogurt sauces and pairs well with other grassy herbs, including basil, dill, chervil, mint, and parsley. It goes nicely with olive, peanut, and sesame oils and oily nuts such as Brazil nuts, cashews, macadamias, and peanuts.

HOW TO USE

To take advantage of cilantro's bright, fresh flavor, add it just before serving. Although it is heartier than chervil, it will still wilt.

Cooked, cilantro turns into an unappealing dark green stringy mess. However, cilantro can enhance flavor during the cooking process. Add a handful of cilantro to the cavity of poultry or fish when roasting or grilling or include cilantro in poaching or steaming liquid or en papillote. When used this way, the cilantro is not eaten.

Both the leaves and the trimmed stems can be used. For maximum freshness, add whole cilantro leaves and stems to soup or broth or an herb salad. For a more diffused flavor, chop the cilantro and incorporate it into rice dishes or condiments.

To chop cilantro, gather the bunch in your left hand and proceed to chop it in the same fashion as you would chervil (see page 65). To preserve its fresh flavor, give it a final chop just before serving.

Larger leaves can be cut in a chiffonade for a delicate presentation (see page 49); however, you probably will not be able to roll the leaves as you can with basil due to size. Cilantro's lacy pale purple flowers are a gorgeous touch to dishes but are usually only available in the springtime.

CHUNKY VEGETABLE GAZPACHO WITH FRESH HERBS

In southern Spain, gazpacho is a chilled soup with a tomato base. It is served in the summer months when tomatoes are the most flavorful and appetites are lighter. (In France, though, gazpacho refers to any chilled soup and can be made with a number of ingredients, including summer fruit.) Gazpacho is often puréed, but I leave this version chunky to show off the fresh herbs, diced vegetables, and garlicky croutons. The jalapeño makes this soup spicy, so omit it if you are serving the soup to children. Be sure to wash your hands after touching the jalapeño and avoid touching your eyes!

2 pounds (900 g) flavorful summer tomatoes	½ teaspoon lemon zest
¾ cup (105 g) seeded and diced Persian cucumber	½ teaspoon lime zest
½ cup (75 g) halved heirloom cherry tomatoes, various colors	¼ cup (4 g) chopped cilantro, stems removed, plus more for garnish
⅓ cup (30 g) diced fennel heart	1 to 2 tablespoons (15 to 28 ml) fresh lemon juice
¾ cup (120 g) diced sweet onion	1½ teaspoons sherry vinegar
1 clove of garlic, minced	¼ cup (60 ml) olive oil, or more as needed
1 scallion, trimmed and chopped	½ teaspoon gros sel de Guérande or sea salt
⅓ cup (50 g) diced red bell pepper	1 avocado, peeled, seeded, and diced, for garnish
⅓ cup (50 g) diced yellow bell pepper	Marjoram leaves, for garnish
1 small jalapeño pepper, seeded and minced	3 cups (150 g) croutons (recipe follows)

Cut any large tomatoes into quarters. Place a vegetable mill fitted with a large disk over a large bowl. Pass the tomatoes through the mill. You should get about 1½ cups (355 ml) juice.

Add the cucumber, cherry tomatoes, fennel, onion, garlic, scallion, red and yellow bell peppers, jalapeño, lemon and lime zests, cilantro, lemon juice, sherry vinegar, olive oil, and sea salt and stir to combine. Adjust the consistency with water if the tomato juice is too thick. (If your tomatoes don't have the taste you thought they would, add a little tomato paste to bump up the flavor.) Add more olive oil as needed for consistency and flavor.

Place in the refrigerator for at least 24 hours. Serve in a chilled bowl. Garnish with the diced avocado, cilantro, marjoram, and croutons.

YIELD: 4 SERVINGS

CROUTONS

3 cups (150 g) stale French or country bread, cut into 1-inch (2.5 cm) cubes

1 clove of garlic, finely minced

1 to 2 tablespoons (15 to 28 ml) olive oil

⅛ teaspoon kosher salt

Preheat the oven to 300°F (150°C, or gas mark 2). Line a baking sheet with parchment paper.

Place the bread cubes in a bowl. Add the garlic, olive oil, and salt. Toss to coat the bread. Spread the bread cubes on the prepared baking sheet. Bake until golden brown, about 10 minutes. Remove from the oven and let cool. These can be made ahead and stored in an airtight container.

YIELD: 3 CUPS (150 G)

GUACAMOLE AND CONFIT DUCK TACOS

This recipe is a marriage of French and Mexican flavors bound by fresh cilantro, which both countries use, though in different ways. This recipe is an example of how to use any of those leftover confit duck legs. If you don't want to use duck, you can use grilled seafood; shredded pork, poultry, or beef; or beans.

3 to 6 tablespoons (45 to 90 ml) rendered duck fat or oil, divided

6 small white corn tortillas

6 confit duck legs (page 62)

6 tablespoons (84 g) guacamole (recipe follows)

¼ cup (18 g) finely shredded red cabbage

¾ cup (54 g) finely shredded green cabbage

¼ cup (28 g) finely grated carrot

Cilantro leaves (and flowers, if available), for garnish

Place a skillet over a medium-high heat. When the skillet is hot, add 1 to 2 tablespoons (15 to 28 ml) of the duck fat. Once hot, add 2 or 3 tortillas and fry on both sides for 2 to 3 minutes until they begin to crisp and bubble a little. Use tongs to remove the tortillas from the pan and place on paper towels. Fold the tortilla in half to shape, blotting with the paper towels to absorb the oil. Repeat for the remaining tortillas. Let cool.

Remove the duck meat from the bones. (Be careful because a few of the bones are delicate and may come off with the meat.) Shred the meat with your hands. To warm the meat, place a dollop of duck fat in a pan over medium heat and add the meat, tossing in the fat until the meat is warm. Remove from the heat.

Once the shells are cool, place 1 tablespoon (14 g) of the guacamole in each one. Add some of the cabbages, carrot, and shredded duck meat. Garnish with the cilantro.

YIELD: 6 TACOS

GUACAMOLE

2 ripe avocados

1 clove of garlic, minced

5 teaspoons (25 ml) fresh lime juice

½ cup (120 ml) olive oil

Pinch of piment d'espelette

½ teaspoon kosher salt

⅛ teaspoon freshly ground pepper

¼ cup (4 g) cilantro leaves

1 tablespoon (10 g) finely minced red onion

Remove the skins and pits from the avocados and discard. Place the avocado flesh in a mini food processor with the garlic, lime juice, olive oil, piment d'espelette, salt, and pepper. Purée until smooth. Add the cilantro and purée again. Stir in the onion. Adjust the seasoning to taste.

YIELD: 1½ CUPS (340 G)

PHO

Poule au pot is a French country dish in which a whole chicken is cooked in a pot with vegetables, creating a flavorful broth. To me, Vietnamese pho (pronounced "fuh") is similar, with a tangier broth served with glass noodles and hordes of fresh herbs. This recipe is a shortcut combination of both. The mix of brandy, garlic, fresh ginger, chicken, greens, and herbs results in a satisfying and delicious broth. Don't rush cooking the vegetables in the beginning and be sure to cook all of the brandy out of the pot. Both steps result in a much more flavorful dish. Serve with lots of fresh herbs, lime wedges, and sliced jalapeños.

4 organic chicken breasts with skin, ribs removed (about 1½ pounds, or 680 g)

Kosher salt and freshly ground black pepper, as needed

2 tablespoons (28 ml) olive oil

½ ounce (15 g) fresh ginger, peeled

1 head of garlic, peeled

1 yellow onion, sliced

1 carrot, sliced

1 celery stalk, sliced

2 tablespoons (28 ml) brandy

1 bay leaf

1 lemongrass stalk (4 inches, or 10 cm), cut into 2 pieces

6 cups (1.4 L) quality chicken stock

1 head of bok choy, leaves separated and halved

1 cup (70 g) sliced mushrooms

Handful of baby spinach leaves

2 or 3 jalapeño peppers, seeded and sliced

Lime wedges, for serving

Baby scallions, for serving

Thai basil, for serving

Sweet basil, for serving

Cilantro, for serving

Season the chicken breasts with salt and pepper. Set aside.

Place a large stockpot over medium heat and add the olive oil. Once the oil is warm, add the ginger, garlic, and onion and sauté until tender, 4 to 5 minutes. Add the carrot and celery and sauté until the onions are translucent and the celery is soft, 3 to 4 minutes. Add the brandy, stir to coat the vegetables, and sauté until the brandy is cooked out of the pan, about 2 minutes. Add the chicken, bay leaf, lemongrass, and chicken stock. Simmer for about 1 hour.

Remove the chicken with tongs, place on a plate, and cover with foil to keep warm. Reduce the chicken stock by one-third. It will take about 10 minutes. Use a spoon to skim any impurities off the top of the stock.

Remove the garlic, bay leaf, lemongrass, and ginger and discard. Add the bok choy, mushrooms, and spinach to the stock and cook for 5 minutes. Adjust the seasoning to taste.

Remove and discard the skin from the chicken. Slice the chicken breasts and divide among 4 to 6 bowls. Ladle the stock and vegetables over the chicken.

Serve with a generous platter filled with sliced jalapenos, lime wedges, baby scallions, Thai and sweet basil, and cilantro.

YIELD: 4 TO 6 SERVINGS

SKIRT STEAK WITH CHIMICHURRI

Chimichurri is both a marinade and a sauce from Argentina served with grilled steak. Traditionally, it is made of parsley and oregano, but I use marjoram and cilantro to bring an unparalleled freshness to this dish. You can substitute other cuts of meat, such as a hanger steak, but always serve it sliced to take advantage of the sauce. For vegetarians, the sauce goes well with large slices of roasted cauliflower or pan-fried medium-firm tofu. Simply place the sauce in a sauté pan, add the roasted cauliflower or diced tofu, and toss in the sauce.

2 cloves of garlic, minced	3 tablespoons (45 ml) Xérès or sherry vinegar
½ cup (8 g) finely chopped cilantro	½ teaspoon lime zest
¼ cup (15 g) finely minced Italian parsley	½ teaspoon red pepper flakes
1 tablespoon (6 g) minced marjoram	½ to 1 teaspoon gros sel de Guérande or sea salt
1 tablespoon (15 ml) fresh lemon juice	1 pound (455 g) skirt steak
½ cup (120 ml) olive oil	Kosher salt and freshly ground pepper, as needed

Combine the garlic, herbs, lemon juice, olive oil, vinegar, lime zest, red pepper flakes, and sea salt in a bowl. Set aside.

Pour one-third of the sauce into a sealable plastic bag. Add the meat. Seal the bag and place in the refrigerator to marinate for 3 hours.

Remove the meat from the refrigerator and let it come to room temperature. Remove from the marinade and wipe off the excess. Discard the marinade in the bag. Season the meat with kosher salt and pepper.

Preheat a grill (or broiler) on high. Turn the heat down to medium-high. Grill the steak for about 5 minutes on each side. Let the meat rest for 10 minutes.

Slice the meat against the grain on the diagonal. Spoon the remaining chimichurri sauce over the meat and serve.

YIELD: 4 SERVINGS

Chicken Milanese with Dill Salsa Verde, page 84

IN THE KITCHEN

DILL

With feathery, small, wispy leaves that resemble carrot tops, this grassy herb has a fresh, clean taste that is readily recognizable. It tastes a little like cucumbers or celery, but overall the taste is so unique and distinctive that it can only be described as "dill."

Dill is prevalent in American, Scandinavian, Turkish, Russian, Persian, and Middle Eastern cuisines. You will also find it used routinely in Mediterranean cuisine. (I love tzatziki, a Greek yogurt-based cucumber-dill sauce served with flat bread and lamb.) The French use dill, too, most often in the Alsace region, which borders Germany.

PAIRINGS

The clean taste of dill is a nice companion to many proteins, including beef, lamb, duck, pork, eggs, poultry, and seafood. It is used most often with salmon, smoked salmon, smoked trout, tuna, shrimp, and scallops.

I like dill in cold grain salads made of bulgur, quinoa, or farro and in legume salads. (Fava beans, lima beans, peas, and Puy lentils are best.) It is also wonderful in cold preparations such as slaws made with kohlrabi, carrot, radish, or cabbage and salads made with carrots, cucumber, potato, zucchini, or mushrooms. Dill also pairs well with sweet vegetables, such as beets, carrots, and red onions, and with vegetables with citrus overtones, such as asparagus, artichokes, and fennel.

Dill brings a cleanness to salads using all types of greens—from soft and watery to those with a little bitterness to them, such as sorrel, escarole, radicchio, and arugula. It also freshens starchy dishes: creamy soups, pastas, risotto, rice, egg noodles, gnocchi, Israel couscous, and orzo. Minced dill can be incorporated into biscuits, crackers, cornbread, scones, popovers, herb breads, and egg dishes.

Try combining dill with various fruits, including tomatoes, summer squash, eggplants, pomegranate, olives, avocado, and berries (mulberries, blueberries, boysenberries, and strawberries). Or use fresh dill with citrus supremes or in a vinaigrette, using the juice from oranges, blood oranges, lemons, limes, or grapefruit.

In terms of dairy, dill is commonly paired with crème fraîche, sour cream, cream cheese, yogurt, mayonnaise, and cheeses ranging from salty feta to semi-firm Cheddar, fontina, Havarti, and Gouda. The combination of dill and Cheddar alone offers many possibilities from omelets to biscuits.

Dill is common in condiments. It does well with mustards, vinegars, capers, caper berries, pickles, and olive oil. For a quick dip or dressing, add dill to crème fraîche or mayonnaise with a little lemon juice and pinch of salt.

Other herbs with cool flavors—lemon thyme, mint, lemongrass, Italian parsley, cilantro, and chervil—go well with dill. Dill also complements sunflower seeds, chia seeds, pumpkin seeds, cashews, macadamia nuts, pine nuts, pistachios, and walnuts.

HOW TO USE

Sprigs of dill should be added just before serving if the dish is warm, but most often the sprigs are incorporated into cold preparations. Similar to cilantro, dill can be added during the cooking process to enhance roasting, steaming, or poaching.

The stems of dill are often thick and not eaten. The more tender ones are fine to eat. The feathery leaves can be plucked from the stems or stripped from the stem. To chop dill, chop in a bunch as you would for chervil (see page 65). Don't chop the pieces too small or the dill flavor will be lost.

CHICKEN MILANESE WITH DILL SALSA VERDE

This classic Italian paillard recipe is usually paired with pasta and diced tomatoes with basil. This recipe pairs the pounded chicken breasts with my version of a salsa verde. The salsa can be stored and used with fish or with pork or beef tenderloin. The salsa can also be puréed and tossed with hot pasta. Although the salsa has many components, it is the dill that gives it its unique flavor. I like to serve a dollop of crème fraîche on the side with this dish. The salsa verde with the warm meat and cool dairy is a delicious texture and flavor combination.

4 chicken breasts, skinless, boneless, and without tenderloin

1½ teaspoons kosher salt, plus more for seasoning chicken

¼ teaspoon freshly ground black pepper, plus more for seasoning chicken

2 tablespoons (8 g) chopped Italian parsley

4 cloves of garlic, minced

Juice from 1 lemon

Olive oil, as needed

1 cup (125 g) all-purpose flour

3 eggs, beaten

1½ cups (175 g) Italian bread crumbs

¼ cup (25 g) grated Parmesan cheese

Crème fraîche, as needed

Lay the chicken breasts (one at a time) in between two sheets of plastic wrap on top of a cutting board. Using a meat mallet, carefully pound the breast to a uniform ¼-inch (6 mm) thickness. Season as needed with salt and pepper and place the pounded breasts in a rimmed dish. Add the parsley, garlic, and lemon juice. Toss to coat. Add enough olive oil to coat the chicken. Marinate in the refrigerator for 3 hours.

Let the meat come to room temperature. Remove from the marinade and wipe off the excess.

To prepare a dredging station, place the flour in one dish and the mixed eggs in a second dish. In a third dish, combine the bread crumbs with the 1½ teaspoons salt, ¼ teaspoon pepper, and Parmesan cheese. Dredge one chicken breast in the flour. Remove and tap off the excess. Then dredge the same breast in the eggs, gently shaking off the excess. Lastly, dredge the chicken in the bread crumb combination, tapping off the excess. Repeat with the remaining 3 breasts.

Place a frying pan over high heat and add olive oil. (There should be a thin, even amount of olive oil across the pan.) When the oil is hot, lower the heat to medium and add a chicken breast. Cook until golden brown, about 3 to 5 minutes, and then flip over and cook until the other side is golden brown and the chicken is cooked all the way through, another 3 to 5 minutes. Place the chicken on a plate and cover loosely with aluminum foil to keep warm while you fry the remaining breasts. If the oil begins to discolor, pour it out, wipe out the pan with paper towels, and add fresh oil to the pan.

Serve with the salsa and crème fraîche.

YIELD: 4 SERVINGS

SALSA VERDE

6 tablespoons (52 g) capers, rinsed and drained

2 tablespoons (11 g) finely chopped fennel bulb

2 tablespoons (20 g) finely chopped white onion

2 tablespoons (8 g) coarsely chopped dill

1 tablespoon (1 g) coarsely chopped cilantro

2 tablespoons (8 g) coarsely chopped Italian parsley

5 tablespoons (75 ml) quality olive oil

2 teaspoons fresh lemon juice

Gros sel de Guérande or sea salt, as needed

Combine the capers, fennel, onion, herbs, olive oil, and lemon juice in a small bowl. Add salt to taste.

YIELD: 1 CUP (240 G)

(LAZY) SUNDAY BRUNCH SMOKED SALMON PLATE

Dill, smoked salmon, and dairy (here, whipped cream cheese) are a classic combination. This is a great dish for brunch when you want to do something special but don't have a lot of time.

4 tablespoons (50 g) whipped cream cheese

2 teaspoons minced dill, plus whole sprigs, for serving

Squeeze of fresh lemon juice

1 pound (455 g) smoked Scottish salmon, sliced

2 tablespoons (20 g) red onion, diced small

2 tablespoons (17 g) cucumbers, diced small

2 tablespoons (17 g) capers, drained and rinsed

2 teaspoons minced chives

Salmon eggs, for serving (optional)

Quality olive oil, as needed

Gros sel de Guérande or sea salt, as needed

Freshly ground black pepper, as needed

In a small bowl, whip the cream cheese with a whisk. Add the dill and lemon juice. Blend well. Set aside.

Place the salmon slices across a large serving plate or individual plates. Add the onion, cucumber, capers, chives, dill sprigs, and salmon eggs in a beautiful way. Drizzle with olive oil and add a sprinkle of salt and pepper. Serve with the whipped cream cheese.

YIELD: 2 TO 4 SERVINGS

TOFU SALAD TARTINE

This mimics an egg salad sandwich. I made it for my daughters one afternoon in lieu of the customary egg version because one of them doesn't care for eggs. A tartine is simply an open-faced sandwich. I usually pair two or three tartines with a small salad or cup of soup for a light lunch or an after school snack.

1 Persian cucumber

6 tablespoons (90 g) crème fraîche

1 tablespoon (4 g) minced dill, plus whole sprigs, for garnish

1 teaspoon minced Italian parsley

½ teaspoon kosher salt

2 to 3 teaspoons (10 to 15 g) Dijon mustard

¼ teaspoon piment d'espelette

¼ teaspoon finely ground black pepper

10 ounces (280 g) semi-firm tofu, diced small

6 slices of sandwich bread

Remove the ends and the seeds of the cucumber and discard. Cut several slices of cucumber for garnish, reserve, and dice the remaining cucumber. Place the crème fraîche, diced cucumber, minced dill, parsley, salt, mustard, piment d'espelette, and pepper in a bowl and stir to combine. Add the tofu and stir to combine. Adjust the seasoning to taste. The tofu salad may be stored in the refrigerator for a few days.

Cut the crusts off of the bread. Cut each slice into two rectangles. Add a spoonful of tofu salad to each one. Garnish with the reserved sliced cucumbers and dill sprigs in a beautiful way.

YIELD: 12 TARTINES

VENETIAN SEAFOOD EN PAPILLOTE

En papillote uses parchment paper to trap moisture and steam the food inside. It is an easy way to prepare seafood, especially for those who may have not had much luck with cooking seafood in the past. I had a version of this in Venice, a city known for its fresh seafood. It inspired me to use dill as a flavor enhancer. Here, the fresh herbs and garlic infuse the moisture with delicate flavor but leave the seafood the star.

12 mussels

12 littleneck clams

12 white shrimp

6 to 7 ounces (170 to 200 g) monkfish fillet, diced into 1-inch (2.5 cm) medallions

12 to 16 cherry tomatoes, various colors

3 cloves of garlic, thinly sliced

1 large shallot, thinly sliced

12 basil leaves

Handful of dill

12 chives, chopped into 1-inch (2.5 cm) pieces

3 tablespoons (12 g) roughly chopped Italian parsley

12 baby scallions, trimmed and cut into 2-inch (5 cm) pieces

1 tablespoon (15 ml) white wine

2 tablespoons (28 ml) olive oil

2 tablespoons (28 g) maître d'hôtel butter (page 103)

Gros sel de Guérande or sea salt, as needed

Freshly ground black pepper, as needed

4 bay leaves

Lemon wedges, for serving

Preheat the oven to 375°F (190°C, or gas mark 5).

Scrub the mussels and clams well. Remove the shells from the shrimp and devein, leaving the tails on. Place all the seafood in a bowl. Add the tomatoes, garlic, shallot, basil, dill, chives, parsley, scallions, wine, and olive oil. Toss to combine.

Place 4 sheets of parchment paper (approximately 16 x 18 inches, or 40.6 x 45.7 cm) on a flat surface. Place ½ tablespoon of the maître d'hôtel butter on each sheet. Add one-fourth of the seafood mixture (with an even distribution of seafood types and herbs), a little salt and pepper, and a bay leaf. Gather the edges of the paper together (leave no open gaps) and tie closed with kitchen twine. Make sure that you tie it tightly and create a seal, allowing no steam to escape. Repeat with the remaining 3 sheets.

Place the 4 paper sacks on a rimmed baking sheet and place in the oven. Bake for 20 minutes. The bags will be toasty brown.

Carefully remove from the oven and place one seafood sack in a shallow bowl. Serve, cutting the parchment just below the string in front of the guest (be careful of the escaping steam). Voilà! Serve with the lemon wedges.

YIELD: 4 SERVINGS

IN THE KITCHEN

FRENCH TARRAGON

French tarragon is grassy herb with a fresh peppery and slightly licorice taste. Its flavor and aroma are distinctive, but too much can easily dominate a dish, so it should be used in moderation.

The French are quite fond of using tarragon. The Italians use it as well, but not to the extent that the French do.

PAIRINGS

Due to its spiky, fresh flavor, tarragon works particularly well with lighter proteins: rabbit, veal, game birds, chicken, seafood (salmon, tuna, sea bass, cod, sole, monkfish, scallops, shrimp, lobster, mussels, and clams), and even eggs. (Deviled eggs are a favorite.) Beef, veal, and pork all pair with tarragon, but here the herb is best served in an accompanying sauce. Tarragon is wonderful in pasta and gnocchi and can be added to other starchy food such as rice.

Cold potato dishes are a popular companion for tarragon and green spring vegetables, such as fennel, asparagus, and artichokes. Tarragon's peppery taste goes well with morels, mushrooms, carrots, parsnips, corn, beets, onions, shallots, and leeks. Fresh tarragon leaves are delicious in salads, particularly those with soft greens, such as butter lettuce, mâche, spinach, and mesclun.

Summer stone fruits and melons, including nectarines, apricots, cherries, peaches, cantaloupe, musk-melon, and honeydew, are a treat with tarragon. Crisp apples, pears, and per-simmons go well with tarragon, too.

Tarragon is often used to flavor oils (olive or walnut oil) and vinegars (Champagne, white or red wine). Tarragon can be used in sauces such as in a brandy reduction with seafood pasta or in a white wine–cream sauce for meat and fish.

Tarragon makes its presence known. The herb turns hollandaise sauce into tangy béarnaise. Add tarragon to deviled eggs and they taste a little more devilish. Raw leaves, whole or minced, bring a new dimension to Dijon mustard, mayonnaise, crème fraîche, sour cream, yogurt, and butter.

Chopped tarragon is generally not used in cooking except in egg preparations, such as omelets and quiche, and savory baked items, such as savory crêpes, cakes, muffins, clafoutis, and cornbread. Like other grassy herbs, tarragon is good with kitchen cheeses and fresh goat cheese.

Citrus (oranges, lemons, limes, and grapefruit) as well as other herbs (basil, chives, chervil, parsley, bay leaf, marjoram, mint, lemon balm, and lemongrass) pair well with tarragon.

HOW TO USE

Tarragon is typically added toward the end of cooking to preserve its fresh flavor. However, it is excellent in poaching liquid or in steaming. Remember to remove the cooked tarragon sprigs before serving, as it turns dark green and limp.

To use raw, strip the leaves from their stems (A). Leaves can be used whole or minced (B). But don't chop the delicate herb too finely; 2 or 3 chops per leaf are enough.

NECTARINE AND HARICOTS VERTS SALAD WITH BUTTERMILK–TARRAGON DRESSING

The use of fresh tarragon in this salad gives a boost to this variation on a peaches-and-cream theme. Serve this for lunch or use it as a side salad. Be sure to use flavorful nectarines. You can substitute apricots or peaches if you choose. If you have flowering chives, use the flowers (sparingly) as a garnish.

1 tablespoon (15 ml) white balsamic vinegar	5 dozen haricots verts
3 tablespoons (45 ml) olive oil	2 nectarines
1 tablespoon (15 ml) reduced-fat buttermilk	⅔ cup (110 g) thinly sliced red onion
½ teaspoon gros sel de Guérande or sea salt	1 tablespoon (4 g) tarragon leaves
1 teaspoon minced tarragon	2 burrata, carefully sliced
1 teaspoon minced shallot	Chive flowers, for garnish

Place the vinegar in a bowl and whisk in the oil and buttermilk. Add the salt, minced tarragon, and shallot. Whisk well until a good emulsion is reached. Set the dressing aside.

Bring a pot of salted water to a boil over high heat. Add the haricots verts and cook for 1 to 2 minutes until crisp-tender. Shock the haricots verts in an ice bath. Drain. Blot dry with paper towels. Set aside.

Wash the nectarines well and dry. Remove the pits and slice into wedges (about 8 per nectarine). Place in a bowl with the thinly sliced red onion. Add the haricots verts and tarragon leaves. Add the dressing to the salad, a little at a time, and toss to coat.

Divide the salad and burrata evenly among the plates. Add chive flowers in a decorative way. Serve chilled.

YIELD: 6 TO 8 SERVINGS

FRENCH TARRAGON POTATO SALAD

The first time I tried potato salad in France I was visiting friends in Provence. I approached it with caution because the potato salad of my childhood was dominated by mayonnaise and scallions and had very little to do with potatoes. However, the potato salad in France had a light, flavorful dressing that let the potatoes remain the focal point. Use small, firm fingerling potatoes with no hint of green.

1½ pounds (680 g) fingerling potatoes

Pinch of kosher salt

1 bay leaf

½ cup (120 ml) quality chicken stock

2 tablespoons (28 g) crème fraîche

2 tablespoons (30 g) grainy mustard

2 tablespoons (28 ml) fruity olive oil

1 teaspoon gros sel de Guérande or sea salt, plus more as needed

2 tablespoons (8 g) chopped tarragon leaves, plus whole sprigs, for garnish

Freshly ground black pepper, as needed

Place the potatoes in a saucepan with cold water to cover; add a pinch of kosher salt and the bay leaf. Place over medium heat and cook until a knife can easily be inserted into the potatoes, about 10 minutes. Drain. Cool. When cool enough to handle, slice the potatoes lengthwise. Place in a bowl. Set aside.

In a saucepan over medium-high heat, reduce the chicken stock by half. It will take about 5 minutes. Remove from the heat and cool. Combine the reduced chicken stock with the crème fraîche, mustard, olive oil, sea salt, and chopped tarragon in a large bowl. Add the potatoes and toss gently to coat. Season with salt and pepper to taste.

The potatoes can be served warm or at room temperature, but they taste best after they have had time to absorb the dressing. (I like to let it sit for 2 to 4 hours.) Garnish with the tarragon sprigs before serving.

YIELD: 4 SERVINGS

BAKED CHICKEN WITH BÉARNAISE

I discovered my affection for béarnaise in college. We served it at the restaurant in which I worked and my favorite thing was to dip french fries into the creamy, tangy sauce. Classic béarnaise is the simple addition of tarragon and vinegar to hollandaise sauce (but some chefs will add parsley or chervil to it as well). It is excellent with vegetables (spinach and asparagus are my favorite), eggs, chicken, veal, and fish. This recipe roasts the chicken with the bones and skin still on, which makes the breast meat more flavorful and juicy. You can use skinless, boneless chicken breasts if you prefer.

2 egg yolks, at room temperature	1 teaspoon Champagne vinegar
1½ teaspoons water, divided	Kosher salt, as needed
2 pinches of cayenne pepper	4 chicken breasts, ribs attached
1½ teaspoons fresh lemon juice, divided	Freshly ground black pepper, as needed
1 cup (235 ml) clarified unsalted butter, warmed (see page 104)	2 or 3 bay leaves
	Olive oil, as needed
2 to 3 teaspoons (3 to 4 g) minced tarragon	

Place a saucepan half full with water over low heat. Place the egg yolks in a nonreactive bowl and whisk rapidly until the yolks are thickened and have the streak appearance of ribbons when whisked.

Place a folded kitchen towel over the top of the pan of water, being careful not to catch it on the burner. Place the bowl of eggs on top of the towel. This is a way to put a buffer between the heat source and the eggs so your emulsion does not break. Add ½ teaspoon of the water, the cayenne pepper, and ½ teaspoon of the lemon juice to the yolks. Whisk well. Slowly drip the clarified butter into the yolks while continuing to whisk very quickly. Continue to add butter a little at a time while moving the bowl back and forth over the water bath, or bain marie, just enough to keep it warm but don't let it get too hot. (If it gets too hot, the emulsion will break and it will look greasy rather than thick and creamy.) Stir in the remaining 1 teaspoon water and the remaining 1 teaspoon lemon juice. Add the tarragon, vinegar, and salt to taste. Remove the sauce from the bain marie.

(If you leave the sauce on the bain marie it will break. Cold sauce will solidify; you can return it to the desired texture by warming a few tablespoons (45 to 60 g) of sauce in a saucepan and whisking it into the rest of the béarnaise.)

Preheat the oven to 350°F (180°C, or gas mark 4).

Season the chicken breasts with salt and pepper. Place the bay leaves in a baking dish, add the breasts (skin side up), and drizzle with the olive oil. Place in the oven and bake uncovered until the juices run clear and the skin is golden brown, about 30 minutes. Baste with the oil periodically.

Remove from the oven and let the chicken rest for about 10 minutes. Remove the skin and rib bones. Slice the breasts on the diagonal. Serve warm or at room temperature with the béarnaise.

NOTE

Should the emulsion break, begin again with a fresh egg yolk, and drip the broken emulsion into the new yolk. Adjust with lemon, salt, vinegar, and tarragon as necessary.

YIELD: 4 SERVINGS

Scallops à la Meunière, page 104

IN THE KITCHEN

ITALIAN PARSLEY

Italian parsley smells like freshly cut grass. It is similar to chervil but is larger in size with a stronger flavor.

It used to be believed that parsley had magical powers. Today, parsley possesses a culinary "magic" in that it brings brightness and balance to a dish, whether it is spicy, fatty, starchy, or lean. Parsley is used in North American, Central American, Spanish, French, Greek, Italian, Moroccan, Middle Eastern, and Persian cuisines, just to name a few. When it comes to savory preparations, the issue isn't whether parsley is compatible with the food, but how much of that grassy taste and texture you want in the final dish.

PAIRINGS

Knowledge of classic combinations using minced parsley is helpful when creating dishes in your own kitchen. Italians use parsley with garlic and lemon zest in gremolata. Parsley, onions, and lemon juice are commonly used in Lebanese cuisine. In North Africa, the combination of cilantro and parsley is used in stews and pastes.

In France, parsley, lemon juice, and butter are responsible for preparations "à la marinière" used with seafood, meats, or vegetable dishes. Eliminating the lemon juice and adding garlic makes a richer sauce (without the tang) that is used in preparations such as in escargots à la Bourguignonne. The combination of chopped garlic and parsley creates "persillade," often added to bread crumbs for gratins or dishes prepared "à la Provençale." Horseradish, parsley, and lemon are commonly used with meats or dairy. Lemon juice and parsley together are great for salads and fish.

Parsley goes equally well with all meat proteins and cuts, including beef, lamb, wild boar, veal, buffalo, pork, poultry, rabbit, duck, and goose. Parsley is instrumental in lightening fatty, starchy, or heavy dishes. Minced parsley is a key ingredient in pâtés and terrines (think meatloaf), ground meat kebabs, sausages, and stuffings. It pairs wonderfully with grains (bulgur, quinoa, and farro), legumes (garbanzo beans, peas, lentils, fava beans, and lima beans), and potatoes (finely chopped parsley is a primary ingredient in pommes Parisienne). Parsley also goes well with lighter proteins such as fish and seafood (calamari, oysters, clams, mussels, shrimp, lobster, and langoustines) and eggs.

Parsley is compatible with a range of vegetables, including carrots, parsnips, celery root, celery, asparagus, artichokes, endives, fennel, potatoes, onions, cauliflower, and radicchio. It also pairs with fruits such as eggplant, tomatoes, winter and summer squash, peppers, and avocados as well as tropical fruits (pineapple, coconut, papaya, mango, and kiwi), stone fruits (nectarines, peaches, apricots, and plums), and autumn fruits (pomegranate, figs, persimmons, apples, pears, and quince).

The herb can be a primary ingredient in marinades, rubs, crusts, salsas, salads, and pestos (alone or in combination with other herbs or greens such as arugula or dandelion greens). It also freshens up condiments such as mustard, mayonnaise, crème fraîche, and sour cream. Parsley is used in maître d'hôtel butter, a pat of which can be used on practically any meat, fish, or vegetable. In Middle Eastern cuisine, chopped parsley is added to vegetable dips such as a moutabel and tzatziki.

Parsley complements mountain cheeses, cheeses ripened on hay, and creamy cheeses. My favorites include Gruyère, Saint Nectaire, fontina, Havarti, Ossau-Iraty Brebis, Brie, and creamy blue cheeses (in a soufflé, for example). It pairs well with both woody and grassy herbs and is part of the fines herbes combination (see page 162) and herbes ventiennes (a combination of tarragon, parsley, chervil, and sorrel used in a beurre manié). Parsley and sage work well together in stuffings and farces, and parsley is wonderful in dairy. Parsley and chives are nice with egg noodles. Chervil and parsley work well on fried vegetables. Use parsley with coriander for a green harissa.

When it comes to baking, I don't add minced parsley to baked items such as savory cakes, crêpes, or gougères because it runs the danger of tasting like hay. Occasionally, I use minced parsley to laminate dough for a savory tart or quiche. Parsley is not really used in desserts because its grassy taste is not as compatible as a minty, woodsy, or peppery-tasting herb would be. If parsley were to be creatively (and minimally) incorporated into a dessert, I would suggest a buttermilk ice cream, a green tea custard, or a cheese tart, something creamy that preserves its freshness.

HOW TO USE
Whole parsley leaves and stems are an integral part of a bouquet garni (see page 60) and used for stocks, soups, simmered dishes, court-bouillon for poaching or steaming, and braises. Like other grassy herbs, cooked parsley turns a stringy, unattractive dark green and should be removed before serving.

Both the stems and the leaves are eaten raw. When using the stems (such as in a salad), use the thinner, more tender stems and leaves.

If you are only using the leaves, pluck them from the stems. For bulk cutting, cut as you would other grassy herbs such as chervil, eliminating the majority of the stems and chopping the leaves in a pile (see page 65). Give parsley a final chop or two right before serving to maximize the "magic" factor.

TERRINE DE CAMPAGNE WITH PARSLEY LAYERS

Terrine de campagne is a rustic pâté, and jambon persil (parsley ham) is a terrine with alternating layers of ham and parsley, bound together with aspic. This recipe is a combination of two. This version is leaner than a typical pâté (which usually calls for a certain percentage of chicken/pork liver and/or straight pork fat). Don't let the "pâté" name fool you, though—this is no more difficult to make than meatloaf. Simply combine everything in a bowl and then alternate the meat with the chopped parsley in the terrine mold. Serve the pâté by the slice with mustard, cornichons, radish slices, caper berries, and crispy French bread. It also makes wonderful sandwiches.

12 slices of unsmoked bacon, divided	¼ cup (31 g) roasted and shelled pistachios
1 pound (455 g) pork butt	Pinch of ground allspice
¼ cup (40 g) finely chopped yellow onion	Pinch of ground nutmeg
1 pound (455 g) ground pork (15% fat)	2 bay leaves, finely minced
2 cloves of garlic, minced	2 teaspoons kosher salt
4 fresh eggs, beaten	½ teaspoon piment d'espelette
2 tablespoons (28 ml) brandy	¼ teaspoon finely ground black pepper
2 tablespoons (28 g) crème fraîche	⅔ cup (40 g) chopped Italian parsley, divided

Preheat the oven to 350°F (180°C, or gas mark 4).

Place 10 slices of the bacon side by side across the width of the mold, with the ends of the bacon slices falling over both long sides of the terrine. Cut the pork butt into 1-inch (2.5 cm) chunks. Don't trim. Place in a food processor and pulse a few times to coarsely chop (don't grind or purée). Remove and set aside.

In a bowl, combine the pork butt, onion, ground pork, garlic, eggs, brandy, crème fraîche, pistachios, allspice, nutmeg, bay leaves, salt, piment d'espelette, and black pepper. Put 1 to 2 tablespoons (15 to 28 g) of the mixture in a pan over medium heat and cook. Taste it and adjust the seasoning in the mixture if necessary.

Spread one-third of the mixture in the terrine. Add half of the parsley on top. Add the second layer of meat. Add the remaining parsley. Add the remaining meat on top. Fold the bacon edges back over the meat. Lay the remaining 2 slices of bacon on top lengthwise over the bacon edges. Place the lid on top. Place the terrine in a large pan and fill the pan with warm water to create a bain marie. (The water should come halfway up the side of the terrine.)

Cook in the bain marie for about 1 hour until the terrine reaches an internal temperature of 152° to 155°F (67° to 68°C). Remove from the oven. The terrine will continue to cook, and you want the internal temperature to rise to 165°F (74°C).

Remove from the bain marie and let the terrine come to room temperature. Place in the refrigerator to set for 24 hours. Unmold the terrine, wiping off the excess fat that has accumulated on the exterior of the pâté. Let the terrine come to room temperature before serving.

YIELD: ONE 12 X 3-INCH (30 X 7.5 CM) TERRINE

MUNG BEAN TABBOULEH

Tabbouleh is a Middle Eastern salad made of parsley, bulgur, and tomatoes. It is prevalent in France, particularly in the south, where the tomatoes are sweet. Tabbouleh is easy to prepare—just chop and combine—and equally delicious with other grains, including quinoa. One day I was experimenting with sprouted mung beans, and they found their way into a tabbouleh. I liked the fresh parsley taste combined with the earthy mung beans, and when I tested the salad on various tasters, the salad got a "thumbs up."

1 cup (52 g) sprouted mung beans	2 tablespoons (28 ml) quality olive oil
6 tablespoons (24 g) minced Italian parsley	2 tablespoons (28 ml) fresh lemon juice
1 teaspoon gros sel de Guérande or sea salt	1 teaspoon Xérès or sherry vinegar

Bring a saucepan of salted water to a boil over medium-high heat. Add the mung beans and gently simmer for about 5 minutes. Remove from the heat and add the lid. Let the beans steam for about 5 to 10 minutes. (This will help the beans hold their shape.) Drain and let cool.

Once cool, add the parsley, sea salt, olive oil, lemon juice, and vinegar. Adjust the seasoning as necessary.

YIELD: 2½ CUPS (575 G)

STEAK FRITES

Steak frites—or steak with french fries—is a bistro staple in France. I have to admit that I think french fries are one of my favorite foods. Give me some béarnaise sauce (page 95) or Dijon mustard in which to dip them and I am pretty satisfied. Here, the french fries are given a fresh zing with chopped herbs, including tarragon, the key ingredient in béarnaise. Generally, french fries are fried twice: first at a low temperature and then at a very high temperature. I like to reduce the amount of frying I do, so in this recipe the potatoes are parcooked in water, dried, and then fried once at a high temperature. If you want to eliminate the frying altogether, toss the parcooked potatoes in olive oil and salt and place them on a baking sheet. Bake them in the oven at 375°F (190°C, or gas mark 5) until golden brown.

4 New York strip (or hanger) steaks

Kosher salt, as needed

Freshly ground black pepper, as needed

2 pounds (900 g) starchy potatoes (Kennebec or russet)

Peanut oil, as needed

4 to 6 tablespoons (55 to 85 g) maitre d'hôtel butter (page 103), divided

¼ cup (15 g) chopped Italian parsley

¼ cup (8 g) chopped chervil

2 tablespoons (8 g) chopped tarragon

Season the meat with salt and pepper. Cover in plastic wrap and place in the refrigerator for 1 day. Remove the steaks from the refrigerator and let them come to room temperature. Preheat the oven to 350°F (180°C, or gas mark 4).

Peel and eye the potatoes. Cut the potatoes to the desired size and add to a large pot of cold water. Bring to a gentle boil over medium-high heat and cook until the potatoes are tender to the touch and translucent, but not falling apart. Drain. Place on a rack and use paper towels to dry well.

Fill a deep fryer or heavy-bottomed Dutch oven half full with peanut oil.

Place a cast-iron pan or an ovenproof large skillet over medium heat. Add 1 to 2 tablespoons (14 to 28 g) of the butter to the pan. Once the butter has melted, add the steaks. Cook until browned on both sides. Place the pan in the oven to finish cooking. For medium-rare, remove from the oven when the meat registers about 125°F (52°C) internally on a meat thermometer, about 8 minutes. Place a pat of maître d'hôtel butter on each steak and as it melts, baste the steaks a few times with the butter. Lightly cover the pan with aluminum foil to keep warm.

Heat the oil to 375° to 400°F (190° to 200°C). Fry the potatoes—in batches (about 2 handfuls) so the oil temperature does not drop too much—until golden brown and crispy, about 10 minutes. Remove the fries from the oil carefully with a spider or fry basket and lay on a metal rack with paper towels underneath to absorb the excess grease.

While still hot, season with salt and the herbs. Serve immediately with the steak.

YIELD: 4 SERVINGS

MAÎTRE D'HÔTEL BUTTER

Maître d'hôtel butter is the combination of butter with salt, lemon, and minced parsley. I always keep it on hand in the refrigerator (it lasts for a few days) or in the freezer, precut into tablespoon (14 g) portions. The butter is often used to braise fish, but it is also delicious on baked or steamed potatoes; steamed, grilled, or sautéed vegetables; and broiled or grilled meats.

1 cup (2 sticks, or 225 g) unsalted butter, at room temperature

2 teaspoons lemon zest

1½ tablespoons (6 g) minced Italian parsley

½ teaspoon gros sel de Guérande or sea salt

2 tablespoons (20 g) finely minced shallot

Combine all the ingredients in a stand mixer fitted with the paddle attachment. Remove the butter with a spatula and form it into the shape of a log. Roll in parchment paper and twist closed on each side. Wrap in plastic wrap.

YIELD: 8 OUNCES (225 G)

SCALLOPS À LA MEUNIÈRE

À la meunière is a mode of preparation using the combination of browned butter, fresh lemon juice, and parsley. The result is nutty, slightly tangy, and fresh. Sole à la meunière is probably the most well-known dish, with trout almondine a close second. This recipe uses the classic preparation with scallops, which are quick to cook and easy to find.

12 large sea scallops

Kosher salt, as needed

Freshly ground black pepper, as needed

All-purpose flour, as needed

1½ tablespoons (25 ml) clarified unsalted butter (see note below)

2 tablespoons (28 g) unsalted butter, cold

1 to 2 teaspoons fresh lemon juice

Gros sel de Guérande or sea salt, as needed

1 tablespoon (4 g) finely minced Italian parsley, plus more as needed

Preheat the oven to 350°F (180°C, or gas mark 4).

Rinse the scallops and remove the foot. Season with kosher salt and pepper.

Right before cooking, dredge the scallops in the flour. Tap off the excess flour. (This is important; too much flour will make the sauce gummy.)

Place an ovenproof skillet or sauté pan over high heat. Once the pan is hot, add the clarified butter so that the scallops will not stick. When the butter is hot, place the scallops in the pan. They should sizzle. Cook for 2 to 3 minutes, just until browned and crispy, and use tongs to flip the scallops and cook the same on the other side.

Add the cold butter to the pan. Use a large spoon to baste the scallops with the melted butter.

Place the pan with the scallops in the oven and cook until the scallops are opaque, 3 to 5 minutes.

Carefully remove the pan from the oven and place it back on the stove top over medium-high heat. Add the lemon juice and season with sea salt and pepper. Add the parsley. Continue to baste with the butter sauce, which should begin to smell nutty.

Divide the scallops among 4 plates, pour the sauce over the scallops, and sprinkle with more parsley if desired.

YIELD: 4 SERVINGS

NOTE

Clarified butter (also called "ghee") is butter with the milk solids and water removed. To clarify butter, place a stick of butter (or more) in a saucepan over low heat and melt. Pour the melted butter into a Pyrex measuring cup and cool. Once cool, you can easily spoon or scrape the foamy milk solids off the top of the butterfat. Poke a hole in the butterfat to let the water, which is at the bottom, escape. This can be done in advance.

Lemongrass Shrimp Kebabs with Green Rice, page 112

IN THE KITCHEN

LEMONGRASS

Lemongrass tastes and smells exactly as it is named: like lemon and grass. It is neither tart as lemon juice or zest nor sweet like lemon confit. Instead, lemongrass adds a dry, grassy-lemon hint to foods but can taste like furniture polish if overused. I include it in the woody herb category, despite its name, because of its hard stalk and because it must be used judicially in cooking.

The first time I encountered lemongrass was years ago in Bali. The cut stalk was used in a spicy coconut shrimp soup. I found the combination so delightful that I ordered it three times in one week.

PAIRINGS

Lemongrass is predominately used in Asian, Southeast Asian, Vietnamese, Thai, Indonesian, Balinese, and Malaysian cuisines. It is used in soups, curries, stir-fries, spring rolls, infusions, and broths. It pairs well with foods common to these regions, such as bok choy (and its varieties), tatsoi, lotus root, Asian radish, Asian greens, ginger, bean sprouts, mushrooms, Thai chiles, Thai basil, and tropical fruits.

Lemongrass pairs well with a full range of proteins, including beef, lamb, pork, poultry, fish, and seafood, especially lobster, clams, mussels, shrimp, scallops, and calamari. It gives a refreshing boost to potatoes, pasta, rice, orzo, couscous, and risottos. Lemongrass can bump up the flavor of kitchen cheeses (ricotta and cream cheese), goat cheese, and other dairy, such as crème fraîche, sour cream, and yogurt.

I like to use lemongrass with lemony shoot and stem vegetables (artichokes, asparagus, and cardoon) and young spring vegetables (ramps, baby carrots, beets, fennel, Tokyo turnips, spring onions, baby zucchini, peas, and shelling beans). It also pairs well with chiles, peppers, tomatoes, scallions, and onions. Lemongrass does well with tropical fruit, such as pineapple, papaya, coconut, mango, kiwi, and lychee, and with citrus.

Lemongrass works nicely with a range of other herbs, especially chervil, basil, cilantro, chives, dill, parsley, mint, rosemary, sage, and thyme. It also goes well with turmeric, ginger, honey, garlic, curries, and vanilla.

Finely grated, lemongrass can give a boost to condiments such as mayonnaise and pairs well with capers, butter, olive oil, olives, and nuts (cashews, peanuts, macadamia, and almonds). Lemongrass can be added to dressings, and it goes well with a range of greens, including spicy greens (arugula and mizuna), soft greens (spinach, butter lettuce, Little Gem, and mesclun), and watery greens (romaine). It can be finely grated and combined with sugar and sprinkled on berries.

HOW TO USE

Lemongrass is constructed like a scallion with a greenish yellow stalk and a slight bulb at the bottom. The bulb and long stalk are usually trimmed before it is sold in your local produce section. The stalk is hard and too fibrous to be eaten as is. To use, cut off the bulb (if present) and trim the top. The remaining portion can be used in one long piece for a gentle lemon infusion. For more lemon flavor, chop the stalk into 2- to 3-inch (5 to 7.5 cm) pieces (A).

Whole or large pieces of the stalk are best used at the beginning of the cooking process. Add the stalk to steaming or poaching liquid. If you serve the liquid, make sure the stalk is obvious so the diner does not eat it. (The hard stalk could pose a choking hazard.)

In cases where the stalk may be hidden in simmered vegetables or you don't plan to strain a sauce or broth, place chopped lemongrass stalk into a tied square of cheesecloth and remove the cheesecloth before serving.

The stalk itself can be used as a skewer (see page 106). You can also finely mince the stalk (B) and add it at the end of the cooking process for a gentle diffusion of lemon flavor, in sautés, stir-fries, soups, salad dressings, sauces, or condiments.

SPRINGTIME VEGETABLE STIR-FRY

This stir-fry screams "spring" with its sweet, young vegetables and bright colors. You don't have to use the vegetables exactly as called for; substitute whatever is freshest. However, there is a particular order to the cooking. The denser vegetables, cut about the same size as an asparagus stalk, are cooked first. Greens or fresh legumes that are less dense and only need to be "melted," rather than cooked, are added later, with the lemongrass sauce. Sautés and stir-fries are the same in that they both use high heat, quick movement, and little fat to cook the food. However, with sautés you make the vegetables jump ("sauter") by moving the pan. In stir-fries like this one, the wok is stationary and the vegetables are moved via tongs or spoons.

1 tablespoon (20 g) honey

1½ teaspoons finely minced lemongrass

½ teaspoon finely grated ginger

1 tablespoon (15 ml) soy sauce

1 tablespoon (15 ml) bottled water

12 baby scallions or 4 spring onions, quartered

12 Tokyo turnips, trimmed and halved, tops reserved

12 asparagus stalks, trimmed and cut to 4-inch (10 cm) pieces

2 or 3 baby fennel hearts, trimmed and quartered

12 baby carrots, various colors, trimmed

1 cup (75 g) sugar snap peas, trimmed

1 cup (63 g) golden snow peas

2 handfuls of Bloomsdale spinach, pea tendrils, and/or reserved turnip tops, trimmed

Basil leaves, as needed

1 tablespoon (15 ml) olive oil

2 cloves of garlic, minced

Combine the honey, lemongrass, ginger, soy sauce, and water in a small bowl. Set next to the stove. Place the scallions, turnips, asparagus, fennel, and carrots in one bowl. Place the snap peas, spinach, and basil in a second bowl.

Heat the oil in a wok or large sauté pan over high heat. Once the pan is hot, add the garlic and sauté until fragrant, about 1 minute, and then immediately add the first bowl of vegetables. Stir-fry by tossing the vegetables in the garlic oil with tongs or wooden spoons.

After about 5 minutes, add the vegetables in the second bowl and the lemongrass sauce. Continue to stir-fry until the greens are wilted, the vegetables are coated in the sauce, and the sauce has thickened slightly, about 2 to 3 minutes. Serve immediately.

YIELD: 4 SERVINGS

SPICY STEAMED MUSSELS IN COCONUT BROTH

Lemongrass goes particularly well with seafood, and I could not resist putting it in this dish. The combination of bacon with lemongrass and spices was inspired by my visits to Bali and Barcelona.

2 pounds (900 g) fresh mussels or clams	¼ teaspoon piment d'espelette
2 slices of bacon, cut into matchsticks	1½ cups (355 ml) dry white wine
2 tablespoons (28 g) unsalted butter, divided	1½ cups (355 ml) unsweetened coconut milk
8 cloves of garlic, thinly sliced	3 lemongrass stalks, chopped into 2-inch (5 cm) pieces
4 shallots, thinly sliced	2 bay leaves
1 or 2 small whole bird chiles	¼ cup (15 g) chopped Italian parsley

Scrub and clean the mussels under cold water. Set aside.

In a stockpot over high heat, add the bacon and 1 tablespoon (14 g) of the butter. Sauté until the bacon is cooked but not crisp, about 5 minutes. Remove the bacon from the pan and set aside. Remove the excess bacon grease from the pan.

Return the pan to medium heat. Add the remaining 1 tablespoon (14 g) butter. When the butter has melted, add the garlic, shallots, chiles, and piment d'espelette. Sweat until the shallots are translucent, 3 or 4 minutes. Add the wine and reduce by a third, about 5 minutes.

Add the coconut milk, lemongrass, and bay leaves. Increase the heat and bring to a boil. Add the mussels. Cover and steam until the mussels open, about 3 to 4 minutes. If the majority of the mussels are open, your dish is done. Discard the unopened ones.

Serve the mussels in the broth. Give the parsley a final chop with a chef's knife and add to the mussels. Serve immediately.

YIELD: 2 SERVINGS

LEMONGRASS SHRIMP KEBABS WITH GREEN RICE

This recipe is just as fun to make as it is delicious. Lemongrass is used two ways: first in the marinade and then as a skewer for the shrimp. This light meal is particularly welcome in the warmer months, and the skewers are a nice variation for passed appetizers at a party. (Try one shrimp per skewer.) The rice pairs with a variety of meat dishes. You can substitute scallops, fish, or chicken for the shrimp, but red meat and pork are too dense for a lemongrass skewer.

2 tablespoons (10 g) chopped lemongrass

2 cloves of garlic, chopped

1 teaspoon ground coriander seeds

1 teaspoon ground cumin

½ teaspoon lemon zest

2 tablespoons (5 g) chopped basil

½ teaspoon kosher salt, plus more as needed

⅛ teaspoon freshly ground black pepper, plus more as needed

Juice from 1 lemon

½ cup (120 ml) olive oil

24 shrimp

12 thin lemongrass stalks

In a large bowl, combine the lemongrass, garlic, coriander, cumin, lemon zest, basil, salt, pepper, lemon juice, and oil.

Remove the shells from the shrimp, leaving the tails on. Devein the shrimp. Place the shrimp in the marinade for 30 minutes. At the same time, soak the lemongrass stalks in water. If the stalks are larger than the size of a pencil, carefully cut them in half lengthwise.

Remove the shrimp from the marinade and the lemongrass stalks from the water. Set the lemongrass on a paper towel to dry. Skewer 3 shrimp on each lemongrass stalk. Season with salt and pepper as needed.

Preheat a grill to medium. Grill the shrimp until cooked through (the center should no longer be translucent), about 3 to 4 minutes on each side. Serve with the green rice.

YIELD: 4 TO 6 SERVINGS

GREEN RICE

2 cups (475 ml) bottled water

Kosher salt, as needed

1 cup (185 g) jasmine or basmati rice

1 tablespoon (3 g) minced chives

2 tablespoons (8 g) chopped Italian parsley

2 tablespoons (2 g) chopped cilantro

1 tablespoon (4 g) chopped dill sprigs

2 tablespoons (12 g) chopped mint leaves

2 tablespoons (5 g) chopped basil

¾ cup (135 g) chopped tomatoes

Place the water in a saucepan with a few pinches of salt. Bring to a boil over medium-high heat. Add the rice, return to a boil, reduce the heat, and simmer, uncovered, until cooked, about 10 minutes. Remove from the heat. Cover with a lid and let the rice steam about 5 minutes.

Add the chopped herbs and tomatoes to the rice. Gently toss and season to taste with salt.

YIELD: 4 CUPS (660 G)

Mint and Puy Lentil Salad, page 121

IN THE KITCHEN

MINT

This grassy herb has a distinctive clean, menthol flavor. Mint's strength and its flavor depends on the variety used, and there are several—spearmint, peppermint, apple mint, and pineapple mint. When a recipe calls for mint, it is usually referring to spearmint, but that does not mean that you should not get creative and try other varieties.

Mint is widely popular because it goes nicely with both sweet and savory dishes, as well as a variety of beverages. Mint is used in Mediterranean, North American, Asian, Greek, Italian, Moroccan, Tunisian, Indian, East Indian, Caribbean, Indonesian, Vietnamese, Thai, Persian, and Middle Eastern cuisines.

PAIRINGS

Classic flavor pairings for mint demonstrate this herb's range: mint with lamb (in England it's a mint jelly, while in Iran it's a lamb and rhubarb stew); mint with yogurt for a dip or sauce; mint with fava beans; mint with ewe's milk cheese or feta; and mint with chocolate.

Mint goes well with a range of proteins, including beef, pork, lamb, game, duck, and poultry. It can be chopped and incorporated into a stew or used in a side dish, pesto, sauce, or jam to complement the meat. Mint pairs well with substantial seafood: swordfish, halibut, monkfish, tuna, lobster, shrimp, and scallops.

Mint lightens starchy foods such as rice dishes, couscous, farro, bulgur, and pasta (both hot and cold) and legumes, including lentils, fava beans, lima beans, garbanzo beans, and haricots verts. It adds freshness to various salads and first courses. Mint is used in fattoush, a Middle Eastern salad using pita bread or flatbread. It is also part of sabzi khordan, an Iranian appetizer combining fresh herbs with onions, radishes, feta, and cucumbers.

It is also perfect with soft greens such as mesclun, mâche, or butterhead lettuce and a range of vegetables (artichokes, asparagus, cardoons, carrots, corn, beets, mushrooms, and rhubarb). Mint also complements hydrating fruits, such as berries (blueberries, strawberries,

blackberries, and boysenberries), citrus (lime, lemon, and grapefruit), melons, stone fruits (peaches, cherries, plums, apricots, and nectarines), and cucumbers, eggplant, summer squash, and tomatoes. It can add a fresh contrast to foods with warmer flavors, including apples, pears, quince, and pomegranate.

Mint can be used with most herbs, including basil, chervil, cilantro, chives, costmary, dill, basil, Italian parsley, lemongrass, lemon verbena, savory, rosemary, tarragon, thyme, and savory. It is often combined with other herbs in a green salad or pesto. Mint complements pine nuts, walnuts, pecans, macadamia, cashews, pistachios, hazelnuts, and chestnuts.

When combined with dairy, mint adds a freshness to crème fraîche, yogurt, cream, sour cream, and buttermilk. The most common cheeses used with mint are feta, ewe's milk, and fresh chèvre (goat cheese). However, it also pairs nicely with hard cheeses, such as aged Parmesan, and blue cheeses, especially with a little honey or sour cherry or fig jam. My favorite use of mint is with goat cheese and chestnut honey.

Mint combines nicely with vanilla. Mint and chocolate create a multitude of dishes. Minced mint can be combined with sugar, including less common sugars such as date and maple sugar. In beverages, mint can be steeped for tea, hot or iced. It complements the flavors of bourbon (think mint julep), brandy, and cognac and can be added to many nonalcoholic beverages (for example, lemonade).

HOW TO USE

If you want a fresh mint flavor, use mint at the end of the cooking process. Use mint in cold dishes such as a salads and tartares.

I prefer to use mint raw. However, it can be added during the cooking process to meat- or bean-based stews. Like other grassy herbs, some mint can also be added to the cavity of fish or poultry to be roasted or grilled. (Remove before serving.)

Mint leaves can be used whole or in part. Pluck the leaves or strip them if the stems are thicker. The leaves can be torn (A) or, for a more uniform look, cut into chiffonade as you would basil (see page 49).

Minced or chopped, mint is good in sauces, dips, salsas, and pestos. If you intend to add chopped leaves to a dish, give them a final chop before serving. Finely minced mint can also be combined with sugar to sprinkle on fruit for a quick dessert. For a rub on lamb chops, add lemon zest to the mint-sugar mixture.

MINT MOJITO

A mojito is generally made with rum. However, I have always found that vodka adds a clean twist. This mojito, with the addition of fruit and a flavored syrup, is inspired by the Black Mojito cocktail at the Hôtel Plaza Athénée in Paris, where they elaborately decorate it with fresh lime wedges, mint leaves, and blackberries.

¼ cup (24 g) mint leaves, plus whole sprigs, for garnish

2 tablespoons (26 g) sugar

¼ cup (60 ml) fresh lime juice

2 tablespoons (28 ml) blackberry or raspberry syrup

Crushed ice, as needed

3 ounces (90 ml) quality vodka

Sparkling water, as needed

Thinly sliced green apple, for garnish

Blackberries, for garnish

Lime peel twists, for garnish

Pound the mint leaves with the sugar in a mortar and pestle. Don't pulverize them; just break them to release the mint flavor. Add the lime juice.

Pour 1 tablespoon (15 ml) of the syrup into each glass. Divide the pounded mint sugar between the glasses. Add ice. Add 1½ ounces (45 ml) vodka to each glass and top with sparkling water to taste. Garnish with the mint sprigs, apple slices, blackberries, and lime peel twists.

YIELD: 2 SERVINGS

SPAGHETTI WITH CHUNKY TOMATO, OLIVE, AND MINT SAUCE

It seems natural to use sweet basil with tomatoes and pasta; however, mint is also excellent. This is a light pasta that is kid-friendly and quickly made, a perfect midweek meal.

1 cup (96 g) mint leaves, plus small leaves, for garnish

½ cup (30 g) Italian parsley leaves

1 cup (24 g) basil leaves, plus small leaves, for garnish

1 tablespoon (2 g) lemon thyme leaves

5 pitted kalamata or Lucques olives

1 clove of garlic, sliced

½ teaspoon gros sel de Guérande or sea salt

Juice from 1 lemon

1 cup (150 g) halved cherry tomatoes

¼ cup (60 ml) quality olive oil

8 ounces (225 g) spaghetti

½ cup (50 g) finely grated Parmesan cheese

Place the mint, parsley, basil, thyme, olives, garlic, and salt in a mini food processor. Pulse 2 or 3 times. Add the lemon juice, tomatoes, and olive oil. Chop but don't purée. Set the sauce aside.

Bring a large saucepan of salted water to a boil over medium-high heat. Add the spaghetti and cook according to package directions until al dente. Drain.

Place the pasta in a bowl. Add the sauce and stir to coat the pasta. Add the cheese and toss to coat. Garnish with the tender mint and basil leaves. Serve immediately.

YIELD: 4 SERVINGS

PAN-FRIED CANTALOUPE WITH HONEY-RICOTTA AND FRESH MINT

After a recent culinary adventure in the south of France, my car was filled with wine, honey, flours, olives, confiture, sausages, and cheese. On the way back to Paris, I passed through Cavaillon, where I felt compelled to pick up a few of the famous melon de Cavaillon (a type of cantaloupe), just because. A few hot nights later, this dish was created. It makes a lovely beginning course, afternoon snack, or light dinner. It can even be a dessert, omitting the prosciutto. The best thing about this recipe is that even if the melon you chose is not as sweet in taste as you imagined, pan-frying it will sweeten it perfectly.

1 tablespoon (6 g) plus 1 teaspoon minced mint leaves, plus more, cut in chiffonade, for garnish

2 teaspoons honey

1 cup (250 g) whole milk ricotta

½ teaspoon fresh lemon juice

1 small cantaloupe

Olive oil, as needed

6 slices of prosciutto or Iberico ham

Combine the minced mint, honey, and ricotta in a bowl. Add the lemon juice to taste. Set aside.

Cut the cantaloupe into wedges. Remove and discard the rind and seeds. Place a frying pan over medium heat and add the olive oil. Once the olive oil is hot, add the cantaloupe wedges in batches. Fry until lightly browned on both sides. Repeat with the remaining wedges.

Serve with the mint-ricotta mixture and the prosciutto on the side.

YIELD: 4 TO 6 SERVINGS

MINT AND PUY LENTIL SALAD

Recipe photo appears on page 114

Puy lentils are small, dark green, and earthy tasting because they grow in the rich, volcanic soil in Le Puy-en-Velay, France. They also hold their shape when cooked, making them perfect for a salad. If your market does not carry Puy lentils, you can substitute green lentils, but remember that they will cook faster than Puy lentils; be careful not to overcook them or they will turn mushy. Once the lentils are done, drain them so they will not absorb any more water. This salad can be a side or a meal—just add a chicken breast or piece of grilled salmon.

¼ cup (38 g) fresh English peas

1 tablespoon (14 g) unsalted butter or olive oil

1 tablespoon (10 g) small diced shallot

2 tablespoons (19 g) small diced Tokyo turnips (optional)

½ cup (96 g) Puy lentils

2 tablespoons (28 ml) dry white wine

1½ cups (355 ml) bottled water

½ teaspoon gros sel de Guérande or sea salt

1 teaspoon Xérès or Spanish vinegar

1 tablespoon (4 g) minced Italian parsley

5 tablespoons (30 g) chopped mint leaves

Handful of mâche

¼ cup (30 g) small diced celery

Chives, for garnish

Bring a small saucepan of salted water to a boil over high heat. Add the peas and cook for 2 minutes. Remove with a colander and shock in an ice bath. Drain. Set the peas aside.

Place a saucepan over medium heat. Add the butter and, once melted, add the shallot and turnips. Sweat until the shallots are translucent, 2 to 3 minutes. Add the lentils and toss to coat. Add the wine, stir to combine, and cook until the wine has been cooked out of the pan.

Add the water and simmer uncovered for about 20 minutes. Cover with a lid and simmer for another 5 minutes. The lentils should be cooked but still hold their shape. Drain and discard any extra water. Add the salt, vinegar, and peas. Toss and set aside to cool.

Once the lentils are cool, add the parsley, mint, mâche, and celery and toss to combine. Adjust the seasoning as necessary. Serve at room temperature or cold, garnished with the chives.

YIELD: 4 SERVINGS

Potato and Brie Soup, page 125

IN THE KITCHEN

ONION CHIVES

Although I classify chives as a grassy herb, they are really part of the allium family, which includes onions, shallots, garlic, and leeks. Onion chives offer a subtle fresh, onion flavor, without tearing your eyes up when you cut them. The recipes in this chapter use onion chives. Garlic chives, which are sometimes also available, smell like garlic.

PAIRINGS

Chives are as versatile as other alliums. They go particularly well with buttery flavors and creamy textures, including vegetable purées such as mashed potatoes, creamy soups both hot and cold (think vichyssoise), and a variety of cheeses from soft kitchen cheeses to hard, grated cheeses. Some favorite cheeses to use with chives are mozzarella, ricotta, burrata, young goat cheese, crottin de chèvre, Brie, Camembert, Parmesan, Gruyère, Comté, Cheddar, and blue cheese. Minced chives added to butter are a bonus for meats and vegetables (corn on the cob or baked potatoes, for example).

Minced chives add a little punch to pasta dishes. They are especially fitting with perciatelli (and a little

Parmesan and walnuts) because the hollow perciatelli resembles chives.

Chives are a wonderful addition to a variety of salads and salad dressings, from vinaigrettes to creamy dressings. You can incorporate minced chives into salads made of crisp or soft leafy greens, such as butterhead, mâche, mesclun, or romaine, and longer pieces of chives with greens that have a little bite to them, such as tender dandelion leaves, frisée, wild arugula, and watercress.

Pair chives with fresh, hydrating fruits and vegetables, such as peaches, nectarines, apples, pears, apricots, cantaloupes, tomatoes, cucumbers, avocado, onions, leeks, peas, fennel, mushrooms, summer squash, radishes, celery, celery root, squash blossoms, bell peppers, endives, and olives, and with legumes. Chives are an especially good partner for citrus (orange, grapefruit, lemon, and lime) and citrus-toned vegetables such as asparagus, artichokes, and cardoons.

Chives are part of fines herbes combination (see page 162). They also pair well with basil, chervil, dill, lemon verbena, lemongrass, marjoram, parsley, and thyme. The herb is also a good fit with pecans, walnuts, or cashews.

HOW TO USE

Chives are best added just before serving. However, there are two exceptions: when minced chives are added to an egg dish (soufflé, omelet, quiche, or scramble eggs) or included in a savory pastry item such as savory pâte à choux (also known as gougères), popovers, scones, or muffins.

Chives can be used one of three ways: chopped, long, or tied. Chives can be chopped in various sizes (A), but it is important to chop uniformly or it has a sloppy appearance. A fine mince (B) can be used to diffuse a hint of onion in soups, salads, smoked fish, and tartares.

Long chives can be used as a significant component in a vegetable or green salad or a tartare or added as a focal point to a composed dish. Lastly, the flexible length of chives can be used for beauty and function. Chives can be tied around a smoked salmon tartare (page 127) or a vegetable roll (C). A chive can be used to tie a savory crêpe, creating a "purse" canapé, or to tie a bundle of haricots verts or a trio of braised leeks.

If the chives are flowering, the purple chive flowers can be added for a beautiful burst of color. You can use the whole flower or parts of it.

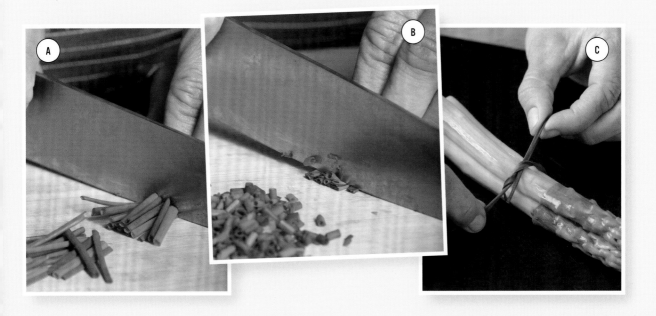

FISH TARTARE

Fresh fish is an absolute requirement for a good tartare. Use a fishmonger you know and trust. Choose a white fish with firm flesh that is a little sweet. My favorites are sea bass, sea bream, and cod. The chives are left in long pieces in this dish for a more prominent flavor.

8 ounces (225 g) sushi-grade fresh fish fillets, skinless

2½ to 3 teaspoons (13 to 15 ml) quality olive oil

Juice from ½ of a lemon

Pinch of piment d'espelette

8 to 10 thin slices of green apple

6 chives, cut into 1- to 2-inch (2.5 to 5 cm) pieces

¼ teaspoon gros sel de Guérande or sea salt

4 to 6 blackberries

Small handful of tender small beet leaves or spinach leaves

Small pinch of freshly ground black pepper

Use a very sharp knife to cut the fish into ½ to ¾ inch (1.3 to 2 cm) cubes. Place in a bowl. Add the olive oil, lemon juice, and piment d'espelette. Toss gently. Add the apples and toss gently to incorporate. Place the bowl in the refrigerator for 20 to 30 minutes.

Add the chives, salt, blackberries, and greens in a decorative, light way before serving. Add a pinch of pepper. Enjoy immediately.

YIELD: 4 SERVINGS

POTATO AND BRIE SOUP

Recipe photo appears on page 122

This soup is a combination of my children's affection for baked potatoes and my fond memories of making potato and leek soup with my grandmother on rainy days. The recipe uses herbs in two ways: you boost the flavor of the soup by sautéing a bay leaf with the leeks and then finish the soup with uniformly chopped chives and bacon.

5 slices of bacon, divided	2 cups (475 ml) bottled water
1 tablespoon (14 g) unsalted butter	1 cup (235 ml) chicken stock
⅓ cup (30 g) chopped leeks (white portion only)	1 ounce (28 g) Brie cheese
2 russet potatoes, peeled and diced	10 chives, minced

Place a saucepan over medium heat. Chop 1 slice of the bacon and add to the saucepan with the butter. Cook until the bacon is softened, but not browned. Add the leeks and bay leaf. Cook until the leeks are tender, 5 to 6 minutes. Add the potatoes, water, and stock. Bring to a boil and then reduce the heat to a simmer. Cook until the potatoes are tender and the flavors come together, about 20 minutes.

While the soup is simmering, trim and cook the remaining 4 slices of bacon in a frying pan or in the microwave. Set on a paper towel to drain. Chop.

Remove the bay leaf from the soup and purée the soup with an immersion blender. Add the Brie cheese and whisk to incorporate. The soup should be the consistency of cold cream. If the soup is too thick, but the flavor profile is good, add a little water. If the soup needs a flavor boost, add a little more stock. If the soup is too thin, continue to simmer until the soup thickens. Adjust the seasoning with salt and pepper.

Garnish each bowl with a generous amount of chopped bacon and chives. Serve warm.

YIELD: 4 SERVINGS

SALMON AND SHRIMP ROULADE WITH CHIVES

When I was in college, I worked in a restaurant owned by a man from the Basque region of France. It was not a French restaurant per se, but the food was certainly French inspired. One of the most popular things on the menu was a salmon tartare entrée served with toast points and a side of very well-braised ratatouille. This dish was inspired by that menu item. I have used this recipe over the years as a passed canapé, and it is always a crowd-pleaser.

8 ounces (225 g) bay shrimp

4 ounces (115 g) smoked Scottish salmon

¼ cup (40 g) diced red onion

4 teaspoons (12 g) minced chives

¼ cup (35 g) diced cucumber

¼ cup (34 g) capers, rinsed and drained

1 tablespoon (4 g) minced Italian parsley

1 teaspoon olive oil

Kosher salt, as needed

2 teaspoons fresh lemon juice, plus more as needed

22 slices of nova lox (smoked salmon slices), each approximately 4 inches (10 cm) long

22 long chives

1 teaspoon grated fresh horseradish

½ cup (120 g) crème fraîche

11 slices of sandwich bread

Chop the shrimp and salmon well with a chef's knife. Transfer to a bowl and add the onion, minced chives, cucumber, capers, parsley, oil, salt to taste, and lemon juice. Mix well. Place in the refrigerator for 30 minutes.

Remove from the refrigerator. Lay 1 slice of nova lox on the counter. Place 1 tablespoon (15 g) of the shrimp mixture on the strip and roll up. Use a long strip of chive to tie the salmon roll closed. Repeat with the remaining 21 slices of lox.

Combine the horseradish with the crème fraîche in a small bowl. Add lemon juice to taste.

Toast the bread, cut off the crusts, and cut each slice into 2 triangles. Serve the salmon rolls with the crème fraîche and toast points on the side.

YIELD: 22 CANAPÉS

IN THE KITCHEN

ROSEMARY

Rosemary, a woody herb, has branch-like stems with green needles that are slightly sticky and smell like pine. If not used judiciously, rosemary can taste medicinal in food.

PAIRINGS

Rosemary is popular in Mediterranean, Provençal, and Italian cooking; it is used as often as basil. Rosemary goes best with sturdy foods and flavors: meats, firm-fleshed seafood, starchy vegetables, and legumes. It is also best in protracted cooking processes, such as simmered legumes, as well as savory baking, roasting, and grilling.

Rosemary works well with most meats: poultry, game, rabbit, all cuts of pork, wild boar, beef, veal, and lamb. Italians often use rosemary with suckling pig. While I like to use rosemary with seafood, it is best when used with a dry-heat source. For example, rosemary is a wonderful addition when grilling or baking whole fish or hearty fish steaks such as swordfish or halibut, but it is too overpowering for delicate fish such as sole. It goes well with starchy foods, including various potato dishes (from roasted potatoes to gratins), rice, pasta, gnocchi, risotto, and legumes. (Fava beans, lima beans, and shelling beans are my favorites.)

I prefer rosemary with vegetables such as onions, carrots, potatoes, and parsnips and hearty fruits, including winter squash, eggplant, peppers, and tomatoes. Fleshy fruits pair well with rosemary, including figs, dates, cherries, peaches, nectarines, apricots, grapes, and olives. I also love rosemary with late summer and autumn fruits: apples, pears, pomegranate, and persimmon.

Rosemary is often paired with citrus, including grapefruit, lemon, lime, orange, blood orange, and kumquat. Classic combinations include lemon, rosemary, and oregano; lemon, garlic, and rosemary; and rosemary, orange, and honey. Any of these can be combined with olive oil and used in a marinade for meats and fish.

Rosemary can be combined with salt and others herbs for a rub or used to infuse oils, honey, vinegars, and syrups. Finely ground with sea salt, it is a great topping for popcorn or other snacks, including toasted nuts (pecans, almonds, pine nuts, walnuts, and hazelnuts). Spices go well with rosemary, especially piment d'espelette, cayenne, paprika, allspice, and cinnamon.

The hint of rosemary is a nice pairing with foods that include some form of alcohol in the cooking process. For example, plums or pears poached in wine or port benefit from a whisper of rosemary in the poaching liquid, risotto deglazed with grappa is delicious with finely minced rosemary, and meat prepared with rosemary is perfect with a jus or a sauce made from sherry, red wine, port, or Champagne.

Rosemary does well with cheese and creams. It can be used with olive oil and garlic to infuse flavor into fresh cheeses like mozzarella, buffalo cheese, ricotta, and goat cheese. It can be simmered in cream to add a hint of flavor. Rosemary also pairs with hard cheeses such as Parmesan. Honey with rosemary is delicious.

Finely minced, rosemary is a wonderful addition to savory baked goods: breads (focaccia, fougasse, or potato bread), crackers, and savory cakes, especially rosemary olive oil tea cake. For sweeter desserts, it can make a refreshing sorbet if it is not overdone. Because of its minty dimension, rosemary is wonderful with chocolate-rosemary ice cream, custard-based desserts (pudding, crème brûlée, and pot du crème), chocolate cake with or without flour, and a variety of yellow and white cakes, including soufflés with a light rosemary cream.

Lastly, a simple rub of rosemary on the inside of a glass can add a refreshing fragrance to a cocktail or glass of bubbly.

HOW TO USE

Rosemary is added at the beginning of the cooking process to draw out the oil in its needles. The stems and whole needles are not eaten. Use a sprig of rosemary when roasting or grilling a whole fish or cut of meat. Small rosemary sprigs can be used to secure rolled and stuffed meats. A sprig of rosemary can be inserted into the cavity of poultry or a suckling pig to be roasted. Small stems with a few needles can be used to lard the flesh of meat or used in baked potatoes or winter squash.

Don't serve whole needles or include them in a product to be eaten, such as a soup, risotto, or baked item. You can eat rosemary in a dish when the preparation calls for stripping the needles from the stem and finely mincing or grinding them. Also, don't add rosemary in stock; it's overwhelming. If you include it in a winter soup (winter squash, potato, or bean), do it judiciously. You can place rosemary in a sachet for simmered dishes; this keeps the needles from being lost in the dish.

The rosemary branch can be used as a skewer. Strip it of most of the needles and soak it in water. You can use it to skewer fresh summer fruits or grill meat or fruit with it. (If the skewer gets charred when cooking meat, you can add a fresh sprig for presentation.)

PARMESAN AND ROSEMARY PANNA COTTA

I love the combination of Parmesan cheese with rosemary, and this dessert—a light, creamy panna cotta—flavored delicately with both, is a heavenly, if surprising, combination. I like to serve it with a drizzle of thick aged balsamic vinegar or balsamic glaze and sweet berries. Make sure that you finely grate the Parmesan cheese. Don't use the pre-grated Parmesan cheese you purchase in the store, because it does not melt as smoothly and can make your panna cotta granular.

2½ gelatin sheets (approximately 2¾ x 9 inches, or 7 x 23 cm)

¾ cup (150 g) sugar

1 cup (235 ml) low-fat (1%) milk

2 cups (475 ml) heavy cream

1 sprig of rosemary, 2 to 3 inches

(5 to 7.5 cm) long

½ cup (50 g) finely grated aged Parmesan cheese

1 tablespoon (15 ml) fresh lemon juice

Fresh strawberries, raspberries, and blueberries, for garnish

Balsamic glaze, for drizzling

Place the gelatin sheets in a bowl of cold water to "bloom," or soften. When they are soft, drain the water and squeeze the gelatin with your hand to remove excess liquid. Set aside.

Place the sugar, milk, cream, and rosemary sprig in a saucepan over medium-high heat. Bring to a boil, whisking occasionally. Once you reach a boil, remove the pan from the heat. Add the cheese, whisking constantly to make sure it is fully melted. Add the lemon juice and whisk again. Remove the rosemary and discard. Add the gelatin and stir until the cheese and gelatin are fully dissolved.

Divide the mixture evenly among eight 2-inch (5 cm) ramekins and place in the refrigerator to set for at least 4 hours.

Run a knife along the side of the ramekin interiors to unmold the panna cotta. Invert the panna cotta in the center of a plate or bowl. Add the rosemary flowers and fresh berries on top in a beautiful way. Drizzle with the balsamic glaze or serve it on the side.

YIELD: 8 (2-INCH, OR 5 CM) PANNA COTTAS

MUSHROOM AND ROSEMARY BEEF TENDERLOIN

Rosemary, olive oil, and garlic are fairly standard in Mediterranean cooking. When I was in college, well before culinary school, I remember reading about a rib-eye roast that used these familiar ingredients, but added soy sauce. I love the combination and have used it throughout the years. I add ground dried porcini mushrooms to give it an earthy, overall woodsy flavor, softening the sharp character of the soy and rosemary. You can substitute a rib-eye roast or a top round roast for the tenderloin, but keep in mind that the top round is a thinner cut and will cook much quicker. Serve this with buttery mashed potatoes, potatoes dauphinoise, or puréed fennel.

4 cloves of garlic, minced, divided	2 teaspoons ground dried porcini mushrooms
2 tablespoons (28 ml) olive oil	2 teaspoons finely minced rosemary
1 tablespoon (15 ml) soy sauce	1 tablespoon (4 g) chopped Italian parsley
1 teaspoon kosher salt	3 pounds (1.4 kg) beef tenderloin, center cut
1 teaspoon coarsely ground black pepper	2 cloves of garlic, thinly sliced

Preheat the oven to 425°F (220°C, or gas mark 7).

Place 2 cloves of the minced garlic and the olive oil, soy sauce, salt, pepper, dried mushrooms, rosemary, and parsley in a mini food processor and pulse to a smooth paste.

Use a thin, sharp knife to make small incisions in the meat and insert the garlic slices. Spread the paste over the top of the meat. Let the meat rest to come to room temperature.

Place the meat in a roasting pan with a rack. Roast for 15 minutes. Lower the temperature to 350°F (180°C, or gas mark 4) and roast for 1 hour to 1 hour 10 minutes longer. Remove the meat from the oven when the internal temperature registers 125°F (52°C) on a meat thermometer. Let the meat rest for 10 to 15 minutes, loosely covered with aluminum foil, before slicing and serving. The temperature of the meat will raise to 130°F (54°C) or a little above, which will be medium-rare.

YIELD: 6 TO 8 SERVINGS

MY NUTTY, CHOCOLATY ROSEMARY COOKIES

My maiden name is Baker, and I think there is something to that because if I have extra time or cannot sleep (usually the latter), I find myself baking something. In ancient Greece, rosemary was used in wedding ceremonies because it was associated with lovers' fidelity and memory. It is also said that rosemary prevents dry skin and fights cancer and Alzheimer's disease. With all of these bonuses, I thought, why not put rosemary in a cookie with . . . chocolate and nuts? This was the result. The cookies will not last long, and the rosemary will not let you forget how wonderful they are.

Heaping ¼ cup (28 g) chopped pecans	butter, at room temperature
¼ cup (30 g) walnut pieces	½ cup (115 g) light brown sugar
1¼ cups (113 g) whole-grain oat flour	½ cup (100 g) granulated sugar
½ cup (60 g) all-purpose flour	1 large egg, beaten, at room temperature
1 teaspoon kosher salt	½ teaspoon finely minced rosemary
½ teaspoon baking powder	1 tablespoon (14 g) vanilla bean paste
¼ teaspoon baking soda	½ cup (88 g) semisweet chocolate chips
½ cup (1 stick, or 112 g) unsalted	¼ cup (44 g) milk chocolate chips

Preheat the oven to 375°F (190°C, or gas mark 5). Line a baking sheet with parchment paper.

Place the pecans and walnuts in a pan and toast the nuts over low heat until golden brown and the oils begin to release. Spread on a plate and let cool.

In a medium bowl, combine the flours, salt, baking powder, and baking soda. In the bowl of a stand mixer fitted with the paddle attachment, cream the butter and sugars until light and fluffy. Add the egg, rosemary, and vanilla bean paste. Mix on low speed. Add the dry ingredients in 2 increments. Mix until incorporated. Fold in the chocolate chips and nuts.

Use a spoon or an ice cream scoop to portion the cookies onto the prepared baking sheet. Bake until the cookies are lightly browned and begin to crack, 8 to 9 minutes. (Don't overbake. The cookies are best soft and gooey.)

Let the cookies cool on the baking sheet for a few minutes and then use a spatula to transfer them to a wire rack. Both the cookie dough and the cookies can be frozen.

YIELD: 1 BAKER'S DOZEN

ROASTED PORK TENDERLOIN WITH ROSEMARY AND FRUIT-SAGE STUFFING

Just when you thought you could not do anything new with rosemary, here comes another idea: stuffing a pork tenderloin with dried fruit, fresh apples, jam, and sage and adding a rosemary sprig so the rosemary flavors the meat from the inside. This is a simple recipe, but don't rush the preparation. You must be very careful when making the incisions in the middle of the tenderloin. Don't hold the tenderloin in your hand while making the incisions in case the knife slips through the side of the meat.

---

1 pork tenderloin (about 1 pound, or 455 g), center cut

Kosher salt and freshly ground black pepper, as needed

¼ cup (38 g) diced dried figs

¼ cup (40 g) diced dried cherries

¼ cup (33 g) diced dried apricots

1 teaspoon dried currants

½ cup (120 ml) hot water

1 tablespoon (20 g) fig jam

¼ cup (38 g) diced Granny Smith apple

1 tablespoon (3 g) minced sage leaves

1 tablespoon (4 g) minced Italian parsley

1 clove of garlic, finely minced

⅛ teaspoon gros sel de Guérande or sea salt

1 long rosemary sprig with a sturdy branch

2 tablespoons (28 ml) clarified butter (see page 104)

Crème fraîche, for garnish

Season the meat with kosher salt and pepper and wrap in plastic wrap. Place in the refrigerator for 1 day.

Combine the dried fruit in a bowl with the hot water. Let soak in the water for a few minutes until the fruit is lightly hydrated. Strain. In a small bowl, combine the hydrated fruit with the fig jam, apples, herbs, garlic, and sea salt. Set aside.

Remove the tenderloin from the refrigerator. Unwrap and let it come to room temperature. Preheat the oven to 400°F (200°C, or gas mark 6).

Lay the tenderloin flat on a cutting board. Hold down the tenderloin by placing your left hand on top of the meat. Holding a long thin knife (a boning knife, for example) in your right hand, make 2 incisions in the tenderloin from the tenderloin end into the center of the tenderloin that will result in an "X" on both ends. First point the blade down in a southwesterly direction (7 o'clock). Insert the knife as far as it will go (about halfway through the center). Withdraw the knife and make a second incision with the blade pointing in a southeasterly (5 o'clock) direction. Repeat the process on the other side. Insert the handle of a wooden spoon gently into the length of the tenderloin to open up the incision. Insert the rosemary sprig into the tenderloin by threading it through the incision (pushing the wooden end of the sprig into the tenderloin first). The rosemary sprig should protrude out a little on each end (it will look like a rolling pin). Use your fingers to insert the stuffing throughout the center of the tenderloin. Try to evenly distribute it as best you can.

Heat the clarified butter in an ovenproof pan over medium heat. Add the tenderloin to the pan and sear on all sides. Place the pan in the oven. Roast the meat for 15 to 20 minutes until the meat registers an internal temperature of 140°F (60°C) on an instant-read meat thermometer. Remove from the oven and cover the meat with aluminum foil to keep warm. Let the meat rest to redistribute the juices. Carryover cooking should raise the temperature to 145°F (63°C).

Remove the rosemary sprig and discard. Slice the tenderloin about ½ inch (1.3 cm) thick. Serve with a dollop of crème fraîche.

YIELD: 4 TO 6 SERVINGS

IN THE KITCHEN

SAGE

Sage, a woody herb, is pungent and smells like camphor with notes of eucalyptus. It has a taste that British cookbook author Elizabeth David described as "altogether too blatant." I like sage, but I agree that it should be used conservatively because overuse will render the dish bitter and medicinal tasting, and common variety sage, rich in two terpene derivatives, is "toxic to the central nervous system," according to food science writer Harold McGee.

Sage seems inextricably linked to some type of stuffing—whether it is Thanksgiving bread stuffing, sausages, or other farce meat. This is because its oily, velvety texture and strong taste balances and is absorbed by fats and starches.

PAIRINGS

Sage enhances the flavor of meats, particularly ground meats that contain fat. It goes well with beef (particularly ground), veal (as in saltimbocca), all types of pork, wild boar, lamb (particularly ground), rabbit, duck, goose, and all types of poultry. If used in moderation, sage is a good partner for egg dishes and seafood, especially heartier textures such as scallops.

Risottos, pastas, farro, and gnocchi–the richer, the better–go well with sage. Italians do an excellent job of giving us examples for using sage, including gently frying the leaves with veal, dipping the leaves in batter and deep-frying them, or finely mincing the leaves and including them in pumpkin ravioli.

Sage's strong but warm personality goes well with the warm, woody flavors of autumn and winter dishes. Brussels sprouts, pumpkin, winter squashes, potatoes, sweet potatoes, mushrooms, and corn are all wonderful with sage. Sage also pairs nicely with the sweet flavors of dried fruit–tart cherries, apricots, plums, figs, and dates–as well as fresh–pomegranate, apples, pears, figs, grapes, dates, and persimmons. Sage and grilled pineapple are often paired together.

Because sage goes so well with fat, it often appears with oils and butter, especially beurre noisette (browned butter). Minced sage can be combined in butter and spread on everything from cornbread to corn on the cob. Sage can also handle the natural fats in nuts, such as hazelnuts, pine nuts, macadamia nuts, pecans, and chestnuts.

The higher the fat content of cheese, the better sage complements it. Look for cow and sheep milk cheeses. If you are in doubt about cheeses to start with, try northern Italian cheeses (fontina, Parmesan, Asiago, Pecorino Toscano, provolone, and Taleggio).

Sage works well in combination with warm spices: quatre d'épices, paprika, nutmeg, allspice, cinnamon, star anise, and juniper berries. Sage is often used in Southwestern cuisine because it goes well with chiles.

Although sage has the potential to work in desserts, it is rarely done successfully for the simple reason that too much of it is used. However, sage can be a wonderful addition to pumpkin, apple, and pecan pies as well as bread puddings (especially those with a little whiskey or cognac in the cream). However, don't use more than one or two leaves or the sage will be the only thing you taste and your sweet note will be lost.

HOW TO USE
Pluck the leaves from the stems. If the stems are thicker, you can strip them as you would rosemary. The stems are never eaten. Sage leaves can be used whole, torn, or chopped. Typically, they are finely chopped.

Sage is best added early in the cooking process so its flavor can be dispersed. Generally, it is chopped and added to stuffings, sausages, or cheese filling for ravioli and then the entire dish is cooked.

Sage is almost never added to moist-heat cooking techniques such as poaching or steaming because it is too overpowering. Used in braises and stews, sage gives a bitter taste and for this reason should never be used for stock or soups. However, used sparingly, sage can be added to hearty dishes with protracted cooking times, such as potato gratins and simmered beans.

A leaf or two of sage can be added to meats or vegetables during the roasting or grilling process. Sage leaves can be panfried or breaded or battered and deep-fried. The leaves can also be used raw in pesto (the cheese and nuts mellow its flavor).

CORNISH GAME HENS WITH FARRO AND SHIITAKE MUSHROOM STUFFING

Farro is an ancient wheat from Italy. Perlato farro is farro where the hull has been removed. It cooks faster and is creamier as a result. If you use farro that still has the hull, soak it in water first to soften it. I usually serve half of a hen per person, dividing the farro among four people, but you could present a full hen to each person.

2 or 4 Cornish game hens	1 cup (185 g) perlato farro
Kosher salt and freshly ground black pepper, as needed	6 tablespoons (90 ml) white wine, divided
	1 bay leaf
3 to 5 tablespoons (42 to 70 g) unsalted butter, at room temperature, divided	2 cups (475 ml) chicken stock, warm, divided
2 tablespoons (20 g) minced shallot	1 tablespoon (3 g) minced sage
¼ cup (30 g) small diced celery	1 tablespoon (4 g) minced Italian parsley
1½ cups (105 g) sliced shiitake mushrooms	Gros sel de Guérande or sea salt, as needed

Pat the hens dry with paper towels. Season inside and out with kosher salt and pepper. Place a teaspoon of room-temperature butter between the breast meat and the skin. Repeat for each hen. Let the hens come to room temperature. Preheat the oven to 375°F (190°C, or gas mark 5).

Place a saucepan over medium heat. Add 1 tablespoon (14 g) of the butter to the hot pan. Once melted, add the shallot and celery. Cook until the shallots are translucent, 2 to 3 minutes. Add the mushrooms and cook until the moisture in the mushrooms has been cooked out, 3 to 5 minutes. (They will be reduced to half their starting size.)

Add the farro and toss in the mixture. Add 2 tablespoons (28 ml) of the wine and stir to combine. Cook until the wine has been cooked out of the pan. Add the bay leaf and ¾ cup (175 ml) of the stock. Once the stock has been absorbed, add another ¾ cup (175 ml) of stock. Cook until the farro is soft, but not mushy, about 30 minutes. Remove from the heat. Discard the bay leaf. Add the minced herbs and season with salt to taste.

Use a spoon to stuff each hen with the faro mixture. You can use a toothpick to close the cavity and keep the farro inside. Use kitchen string to truss the legs together. Place the hens on a rack in a roasting pan. Place in the oven.

After the hens have been in the oven for about 25 minutes, pour the remaining 4 tablespoons (60 ml) wine and remaining ½ cup (120 ml) chicken stock to the bottom of the roasting pan and return the pan to the oven. After 5 minutes, carefully baste the hens with the liquid. Continue to roast until the skin is crispy brown and the juice at the thigh runs clear, about 30 to 40 minutes total oven time. Remove the hens when the internal temperature reaches 162°F (72°C) on an instant-read thermometer. Let rest for 10 minutes until the internal temperature rises to 165°F (74°C), before serving.

Remove the kitchen string. Use kitchen sheers or a knife to cut the game hens in half between the breasts. Serve with the farro stuffing and jus from the roasting pan.

YIELD: 4 SERVINGS

AUTUMN PESTO WITH ROASTED BRUSSELS SPROUTS

Sage pairs nicely with the warm flavors of autumn. While pesto is generally made with grassy herbs or greens, this one combines sage, thyme, and toasted hazelnuts. The idea was inspired by the sage pesto pasta at Zuni Cafe in San Francisco. The hazelnuts and herbs create a beautiful red and green pesto that is a flavorful and festive addition to be swirled in a winter squash soup or spread on roasted vegetables or a turkey sandwich. (It's perfect for Thanksgiving leftovers.) Here, the pesto gives Brussels sprouts a new twist.

1 cup (135 g) hazelnuts	5 tablespoons (25 g) grated Parmesan cheese
⅓ cup (13 g) sage leaves	½ cup (120 ml) quality olive oil, plus more as needed
2 teaspoons thyme leaves	Kosher salt, as needed
1 clove of garlic, smashed	2 pounds (900 g) Brussels sprouts with tight buds
½ to 1 teaspoon fresh lemon juice	12 Medjool or honey dates, pitted and chopped

Preheat the oven to 350°F (180°C, or gas mark 4).

Place the hazelnuts in a pan over medium heat. Toast until the nuts begin to release their oils. This only takes about 3 minutes (do not burn them or you have to start over). Remove and carefully place in a food processor. Pulse until coarse.

Using a mortar and pestle, pound the sage and thyme to a green paste. Add the garlic and pound together. Add the hazelnuts, lemon juice, and cheese. Slowly add the olive oil and combine the ingredients into a paste. Season with salt to taste.

Cut the Brussels sprouts in half. Place in a bowl and toss with olive oil as needed to coat and a few pinches of salt. Place in a baking dish and roast until the Brussels sprouts are tender and slightly crisp, about 30 minutes. Use a wooden spoon to move them during the roasting process so they don't stick to the bottom.

Remove from oven and while warm, add the pesto by the spoonful and toss to coat the Brussels sprouts (you most likely will have some pesto left over). Add the dates and stir to combine. This can be served warm or at room temperature.

YIELD: 8 TO 10 SERVINGS

SALTIMBOCCA

This is a classic Roman preparation of veal using fresh sage. If you don't want to use veal, you can use chicken or pork cutlets, but remember that the cooking time will be longer.

4 veal scaloppine	12 sage leaves
Kosher salt and freshly ground black pepper, as needed	1 tablespoon (14 g) unsalted butter, plus more as needed
4 slices of prosciutto	¼ cup (60 ml) white wine

Use a cutlet pounder to pound the scaloppine so all 4 are an even thickness. Season with salt and pepper. Place a slice of prosciutto on top of each cutlet. Place 3 sage leaves on each prosciutto slice and secure the sage leaves with toothpicks.

Place a pan over medium heat. When pan is hot, add the butter and melt. Add 2 veal scaloppine to the pan, sage side down. Cook in the butter for about 2 minutes. Turn over and cook for another 2 minutes until the veal is done. Remove the scaloppine from the pan and place on a plate. Loosely cover with foil to keep warm. Repeat the process with the remaining 2 scaloppine, adding more butter as needed. Remove and keep warm.

Add the wine to the pan and cook until reduced by half, 3 or 4 minutes.

Place the saltimbocca on plates with the sage side up. Remove the toothpicks. Pour the wine and butter mixture over each one and serve.

YIELD: 4 SERVINGS

◀ *Autumn Pesto with Roasted Brussels Sprouts, page 140*

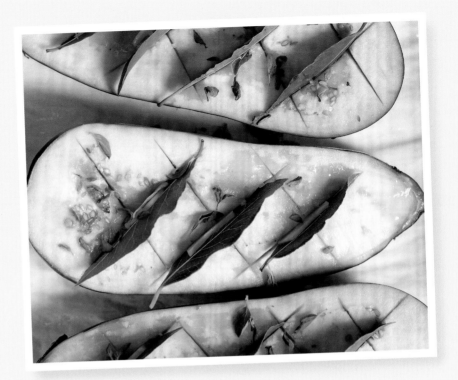

IN THE KITCHEN

SWEET MARJORAM

The soft, velvety feel of sweet marjoram leaves is deceiving; this woody herb packs quite a punch. Sweet marjoram, which is often simply called marjoram in the kitchen, is pungent, with a woodsy and slightly bitter taste. It is often substituted for oregano. Both herbs are in the same family, but marjoram is not as strong.

PAIRINGS

Marjoram is popular in Mediterranean, Moroccan, North African, Middle Eastern, Italian, and French cuisines. When I think of what pairs best with marjoram, I instinctually think of Mediterranean and North African cuisines and late summer foods, including lamb, veal, tomatoes, summer squash, eggplant, peppers, artichokes, cauliflower, sweet onions, olives, and olive oil.

I prefer to use marjoram with stronger meats, such wild boar or lamb, and substantial fish, such as halibut, tuna, or swordfish, because they will not be overwhelmed by marjoram's intensity. However, marjoram's ability to pair with proteins extends to turkey, chicken, rabbit, pork, duck, and goose. It also pairs well with a variety of firm-fleshed fish, although it is too strong for delicate, flaky fish such as sole. It is good with clams, mussels, and lobster. I like it with eggs, too.

Marjoram is delicious in hearty dishes: beef stews with a tomato-red wine sauce, thick bean soups, and braises. It is a flavorful addition to meat and vegetable terrines. Starches such as potatoes, risotto, farro, stuffings, couscous, and pastas, as well as legumes, especially fava beans, shelling beans, peas, green beans, and lima beans, are all good with marjoram. It adds a refreshing note to fresh kitchen cheeses and creams: mozzarella, buffalo mozzarella, ricotta, feta, sour cream, crème fraîche, cream cheese, and mascarpone.

Marjoram pairs well with other woody herbs, particularly bay laurel, thyme, rosemary, and sage, and goes nicely with fresh parsley, mint, savory, and tarragon. Pine nuts, walnuts, almonds, pecans, and hazelnuts complement marjoram, and marjoram can be used as part of a pesto.

I am preferential to using marjoram with certain Mediterranean combinations: marjoram with thyme and/or lemon or olive oil; or marjoram with garlic and/or lemon. I like to add marjoram to confit of garlic, tomatoes, or eggplant. I add raw leaves to salads and braised summer vegetables.

Although minced marjoram can be used in baked items, these tend to be savory rather than sweet.

HOW TO USE
Generally, marjoram is best used at the end of the cooking process. Strip the leaves from their stems and use whole or broken leaves. The stems, although generally less woody then those of other woody herbs, are usually not eaten.

For a more subtle marjoram flavor, use marjoram in the cooking process as part of a less traditional bouquet garni.

ROASTED LEG OF LAMB WITH MARJORAM JUS

This is one of my favorite ways to use marjoram, and the recipe, while impressive to guests, is simple for the cook. If you don't want to debone the leg of lamb yourself, ask your butcher to remove it (but keep the bone) and trim the excess fat. The marjoram and garlic flavor the meat while cooking, but it is the marjoram-infused jus served with the sliced meat that makes the dish.

1 whole leg of lamb

Kosher salt and freshly ground black pepper, as needed

Juice from ½ of a lemon

1 to 2 tablespoons (6 to 12 g) minced

marjoram, plus 2 whole sprigs

6 cloves of garlic, thinly sliced

½ cup (120 ml) red wine

2½ cups (570 ml) quality chicken or beef stock, divided

Using a boning knife, remove the silver skin and large pieces or strips of fat from the leg. Discard. Remove the bone by cutting against the bone and corkscrewing the bone out of the meat. Reserve the bone. Lay the meat open (the sections of meat will spread out like an open book). Season both sides of the meat with salt and pepper. Cover the meat with plastic wrap and place in the refrigerator for 1 day.

Remove the lamb from the refrigerator. Open the meat and sprinkle with the lemon juice and minced marjoram. Roll and tie the lamb leg closed with kitchen twine. Cut small incisions into the meat (or use the spaces in between the natural folds) to insert the garlic slices. Cover the lamb with aluminum foil. Let the tied lamb rest for 3 hours; it should be at room temperature before you roast it.

Preheat the oven to 375°F (190°C, or gas mark 5).

Place the lamb on a rack in a roasting pan just large enough to hold it. Place the leg bone on the bottom of the roasting pan. Roast for about 1 hour to 1 hour 20 minutes. For medium-rare (the meat will be light red), roast the lamb until it registers an internal temperature of 125°F (52°C) on a meat thermometer inserted into the thickest part of the leg. For medium (the meat will be pink), take the meat out when it registers 135°F (57°C). Remove the lamb from the pan and place it on a plate, loosely covered with aluminum foil to keep warm. (The meat will continue to cook.)

Remove the lamb bone from the roasting pan and discard. Pour off the excess fat from the pan. Place the pan on the stove over high heat. Add the wine and 1 cup (235 ml) of the stock, scraping up the bits from the bottom of the pan. Stir until the liquid is largely cooked out of the pan. Add the remaining 1½ cups (355 ml) stock and the sprigs of marjoram. Cook for another 7 to 10 minutes to reduce. Strain through a sieve and discard the marjoram.

When the meat reaches an internal temperature of 130° to 140°F (54° to 60°C), it is medium-rare. For medium, it should reach 140° to 150°F (60° to 66°C). Slice the lamb and serve with the jus.

YIELD: 8 SERVINGS

GREEK SALAD

This fresh and crispy salad uses raw marjoram leaves for a Mediterranean classic. If you want an extra special side dish for your meal, hollow out some tomatoes or large lemons and stuff them with some of the Greek salad. Garnish with marjoram leaves.

1 cup (150 g) halved heirloom cherry tomatoes, various colors

3 Persian cucumbers

¼ cup (25 g) pitted kalamata olives

¼ cup (40 g) diced red onion

2 tablespoons (12 g) chopped marjoram leaves

1 tablespoon (13 g) Greek yogurt

2 tablespoons (28 ml) olive oil

4 teaspoons (20 ml) fresh lemon juice

½ to 1 teaspoon gros sel de Guérande or sea salt

¼ cup (38 g) crumbled feta cheese

1 avocado, peeled, pitted, and diced (optional)

2 anchovies, drained and chopped (optional)

Mint leaves, for garnish

Cut the tomatoes, cucumbers, and olives to about the same size. Place in a bowl with the onion and marjoram.

In a separate bowl, whisk together the yogurt, olive oil, lemon juice, and salt. Add to the salad and toss to combine.

Add the feta cheese, avocado, and anchovies. Toss a few times. Let set for 20 minutes before serving, garnished with the mint.

YIELD: 4 SERVINGS

ROASTED EGGPLANT WITH (GREEN) ZA'ATAR

Roasting vegetables and fruits with herbs is a way to impart the herb flavor in the food as the moisture is cooked out. I recall reading about Chef Alain Ducasse inserting mint leaves into vegetables to be roasted, a technique that could be called a vegetarian "larding." (Usually larding is the insertion of fat into a meat protein.) I thought the use of the herb was genius and it inspired this recipe.

Za'atar, used in Middle Eastern cuisine, is both its own herb and a blend of dried herbs and spices. Traditionally, za'atar is red due to the sumac included in the blend, but my version is green because of its reliance on fresh thyme and marjoram leaves. You can use the za'atar with a variety of meat and vegetables dishes and on warm flatbread.

2 small eggplants	12 bay leaves
Gros sel de Guérande or sea salt, as needed	4 sprigs of marjoram
Olive oil, as needed	

Cut the eggplants in half lengthwise. Use a knife to score the flesh by making diagonal incisions, resembling diamonds. Sprinkle with salt. Set aside for 30 minutes.

Preheat the oven to 350°F (180°C, or gas mark 4).

Drizzle the eggplant halves with olive oil. Place the garlic slices and bay leaves in the incisions made in each eggplant, about 3 or 4 garlic slices and 3 or 4 bay leaves per eggplant half. Top with a sprig of marjoram on each eggplant half. Roast, skin side down, for 30 to 40 minutes, until eggplant flesh is soft and brown.

Remove the eggplant from the oven. Remove the cooked herbs from the eggplant. Serve warm with the za'atar on the side for guests to use as a sauce or dip to their liking.

YIELD: 4 SERVINGS

ZA'ATAR

4 tablespoons (24 g) marjoram leaves	¼ teaspoon kosher salt
4 tablespoons (10 g) thyme leaves	4 teaspoons (11 g) white sesame seeds
1 teaspoon ground sumac	⅓ cup plus 1 tablespoon (95 ml) quality olive oil

Pound the marjoram and thyme leaves using a mortar and pestle. Add the sumac and salt. Combine. Add the sesame seeds and olive oil. Stir to incorporate. Transfer to a bowl.

YIELD: ⅓ CUP (80 ML)

IN THE KITCHEN

THYME

French thyme smells and tastes woodsy, warm, and slightly sweet. The leaves are very small and the stems, which can be thick, are not generally eaten. Lemon thyme smells like lemon but must be used sparingly because it has the potential (as with all lemon-scented herbs) to resemble furniture polish in smell and taste.

PAIRINGS

Thyme is wonderful in traditional autumn and winter preparations, such as braises, stews, and bread stuffing. It also pairs well with summer flavors and is delicious in braised zucchini dishes and ratatouille or with poached apricots. It is used often in Mediterranean and Turkish cuisines and is often a key ingredient in French sauces.

Like other woody herbs, thyme goes well with all meats: veal chops, lamb chops, roasted leg of lamb, meatloaf and meat terrines, sausages, rabbit, foie gras, goose, venison, and poultry. It is especially good with duck, quail, and wild boar. Thyme also goes well in seafood chowders, soups, and stews. Think bouillabaisse and gumbo. It is best with heartier fish prepared using the dry-heat methods of baking, roasting, and grilling, though it can be great in an en papillote preparation, too.

My favorite pairings for thyme are other woody ingredients, such as mushrooms (chanterelles, morels, and porcini), truffles, and chestnuts, and Mediterranean flavors, such as tomatoes, eggplants, onions, summer and winter squash, peppers, leeks, fennel, shallots, garlic, roasted garlic, olives, capers, olive oil, Mediterranean fish, and lamb. Other common vegetable pairings for thyme are carrots, parsnips, potatoes, and celery. Legumes, such as peas, shelling beans, fava beans, lima beans, lentils, and garbanzo beans, are delicious partners for thyme, too.

Try thyme with hazelnuts, chestnuts, almonds, and pine nuts. Cheeses, from kitchen cheeses and baked Camembert and Brie to firmer cheeses such as Parmesan and Gruyère, do well with thyme.

An essential part of herbes de Provence (page 162), thyme generally pairs well with other woody herbs (bay laurel, rosemary, marjoram, savory, and oregano). It can be delicious as part of a marinade or rub for meat with (or without) other herbs, olive oil, citrus, and garlic. Thyme is also excellent with olives, capers, mustards, honey, and vinegars.

Due to their slight tartness, fresh tender thyme stems are a refreshing companion to fruit, whether fresh, poached, or grilled. Try thyme with melon (especially cantaloupe), apricots, peaches, and nectarines. It is good in custards, jellies, and jams, both sweet and savory.

Lemon thyme can be used with most of the foods where you would use French thyme, although it is not as flattering to woody flavors. Lemon thyme does particularly well with baked items but must be used sparingly.

HOW TO USE

Thyme is best used early in the cooking process when stewing, braising, grilling, roasting, poaching, or steaming. Add the sprigs to a bouquet garni (page 60) or, if you add them loosely, pull the stems from the dish before serving.

Thyme leaves are too small to chop. Strip the leaves from the stem as you do for savory and tarragon (see page 91). If the stems are tender, you can add them delicately to a dish as a garnish.

LAMB CHOPS ROASTED ON THYME

Recipe photo appears on page 151

One summer, I lunched at Les Bories (in the Hotel Les Bories & Spa) in the Luberon region of France because I wanted to try Chef Pascal Ginoux's food. One of the dishes was a rack of lamb roasted and smoked on a bed of French thyme. The waiter brought the cooking vessel to the table and when he opened the lid, the smell of thyme and roasted lamb filled the air. I had used mirepoix as a rack for roasting poultry, but never herbs in that fashion. Only later did I learn that it was a technique common in French cooking. Here is how you can use this delicious technique at home.

1 rack of lamb, trimmed	2 tablespoons (20 g) minced shallot
Kosher salt and freshly ground black pepper, as needed	1 teaspoon tomato paste
1 to 2 tablespoons (15 to 28 ml) olive oil	¾ cup (175 ml) red wine or port
3 or 4 bunches of thyme, plus 5 thyme sprigs, divided	1¼ cups (285 ml) beef or veal stock
3 bay leaves	1½ teaspoons ground arrowroot dissolved in 1 tablespoon (15 ml) red wine
1 tablespoon (14 g) unsalted butter	Fresh lemon juice, as needed

Preheat the oven to 425°F (220°C, or gas mark 7).

Cut the rack in half (about 4 ribs on each piece). Season the lamb chops with salt and pepper.

Place a pan over medium heat. Add the olive oil. Brown the top and bottom of the lamb chops in the pan. Do not brown the sides of the meat. Remove the lamb chops from the pan and reserve the pan with the drippings.

Spread the bunches of thyme and the bay leaves in the bottom of a cocotte or Dutch oven. Place the lamb chops on top, meat side up. Cover with the lid. Roast until the meat registers 125° to 130°F (52° to 54°C) on an internal meat thermometer, about 15 minutes. Remove the lamb chops and place on a plate, loosely covered with aluminum foil to keep warm. Let the meat rest for 10 minutes.

While the lamb chops are roasting, pour out the excess grease from the pan in which you browned the lamb and place the pan over medium-high heat. Once hot, add the butter. When the butter has melted, add the shallot and remaining 5 thyme sprigs. Sweat the shallots for 3 or 4 minutes until translucent. Add the tomato paste, red wine, and beef stock, stir to combine, and cook until reduced to 1 cup, about 10 minutes.

Strain the sauce into a clean saucepan and discard the shallots and thyme. Whisk in the arrowroot slurry. Cook until the sauce thickens. Season to taste with salt and pepper and adjust the flavor with lemon juice.

YIELD: 2 SERVINGS

FAVA BEANS AND ENGLISH PEAS WITH THYME

There is something about spring when fava beans show up in the market, the peas are at their sweetest, and the thyme is flowering. The combination of the three ingredients with a little bacon is a wonderful side for any meat dish or can be combined in pasta.

4 cups (600 g) shelled fresh fava beans
(about 5 pounds, or 2.3 kg, in the pod)

¼ cup (20 g) lardons or 1 slice of bacon, chopped

½ cup (75 g) shelled fresh English peas

1 tablespoon (14 g) unsalted butter

1 teaspoon thyme leaves

Fresh lemon juice, as needed

Gros sel de Guérande or sea salt, as needed

Freshly ground black pepper, as needed

Thyme flowers, for garnish

Bring a pot of salted water to a boil over medium-high heat. Add the fava beans and blanch for 1 to 2 minutes. Remove from the boiling water with a strainer and place in an ice bath. Remove and dry. Once cool enough to handle, pinch the skins from the beans and discard. Place the fava beans in a bowl.

Place a pan over medium heat. Add the lardons and render the fat. Add the peas and toss in the fat. Add the fava beans, butter, and thyme. Sauté for a few minutes until cooked to desired doneness. Remove from the heat.

Adjust the seasoning to taste with lemon juice, sea salt, and pepper. Garnish with the thyme flowers.

YIELD: 4 SERVINGS

◀ *Lamb Chops Roasted on Thyme, page 150*

LEMON THYME AND YOGURT CAKE

This cake is perfect for the afternoon. It is light and not too sweet. You can enjoy it with or without the mascarpone frosting. In the summer, make the frosting and serve it with fresh berries for a luscious dessert.

1¾ cups (196 g) cake flour

1 teaspoon kosher salt

1 teaspoon baking powder

½ cup (1 stick, or 112 g) unsalted butter, at room temperature

1 cup (200 g) plus 1 tablespoon (13 g) sugar, divided

3 large eggs, divided

1 teaspoon vanilla bean paste

Zest of 1 Meyer lemon

2 teaspoons lemon thyme leaves

¾ cup (150 g) nonfat, plain Greek yogurt

Fresh edible flowers, for garnish

Preheat the oven to 350°F (180°C, or gas mark 4).

In a bowl, mix together the flour, salt, and baking powder. Set aside.

In the bowl of a stand mixer fitted with the paddle attachment, cream the butter and 1 cup (200 g) of the sugar. Once the butter is pale yellow, add the egg yolks, vanilla bean paste, lemon zest, and thyme leaves. Mix to incorporate well.

With the mixer on low speed, alternate adding the dry ingredients and the yogurt to the batter. First add one-third of the flour. Mix. Add half of the yogurt. Mix. Add another one-third of the flour. Mix. Add the remaining half of the yogurt. Mix. Add the remaining one-third flour. Mix well. Remove the bowl from the mixer.

Use a clean bowl for the stand mixer and the whisk attachment to whisk the egg whites on medium speed. When the eggs are foamy, add the remaining 1 tablespoon (13 g) sugar. Mix on medium speed until soft peaks form and then turn the mixer up to high speed. Whisk until the whites form stiff peaks.

Use a spatula to incorporate one-third of the egg whites into the batter. Fold the remaining egg whites into the batter in thirds.

Pour the batter into the prepared pan, smoothing the top. Place the pan on a baking sheet in the middle rack of the oven. Bake until the top is light golden brown and a toothpick inserted into the center comes out clean, 20 to 25 minutes. Don't overbake. Cool slightly in the pan and then remove to a wire baking rack.

Frost the cake in a beautiful way. Use the edible flowers for garnish.

YIELD: ONE 8-INCH (20 CM) CAKE

MASCARPONE FROSTING

½ cup (120 ml) heavy whipping cream

1 tablespoon (15 ml) pure vanilla extract

1 tablespoon (8 g) confectioners' sugar

½ cup (120 g) mascarpone cheese

Place the cream and vanilla in the bowl of a stand mixer fitted with the whisk attachment. Turn on to medium speed. When the cream begins to thicken, pour in the sugar and turn the speed up to high. Continue to whisk on high until the cream forms stiff peaks. Turn the mixer off. Fold the whipped cream into the mascarpone cheese. The frosting can be stored in an airtight container in the refrigerator.

YIELD: 1 CUP (240 G)

BAKED DAURADE WITH THYME, OLIVES, AND POTATOES AND MINT CHERMOULA

Chermoula is a Moroccan paste often used for couscous and fish. It can be used with rice, chicken, lamb, or beef or served with Stuffed Tomatoes à la Provençale et Maroc (page 166).

1 whole daurade (about 1 pound, or 455 g)

Kosher salt and freshly ground black pepper, as needed

4 Peruvian baby potatoes, quartered

6 caper berries

½ cup (50 g) pitted Niçoise olives

Olive oil, as needed

6 sprigs of thyme, divided

2 bay leaves

Gros sel de Guérande or sea salt, as needed

2 tablespoons (17 g) capers, rinsed and drained

Preheat the oven to 400°F (200°C, or gas mark 6).

Ask your fishmonger to clean the fish and remove the viscera. Season the inside of the fish with kosher salt and pepper.

Place the potatoes in a pan of cold water over medium heat. Cook until two-thirds done (soft but not soft enough to insert a fork), about 8 minutes. Drain and dry.

Once dry, place the potatoes, caper berries, and olives in a bowl and toss to coat with the oil from the olives, adding more olive oil as needed. Place in a baking dish.

Stuff the cavity of the fish with 2 of the thyme sprigs and the bay leaves and place the whole fish in the baking dish on top of the potato mixture. Drizzle olive oil over the fish. Sprinkle with sea salt and 2 of the thyme sprigs. Transfer to the oven and bake for 25 minutes.

Garnish with the capers and the remaining 2 thyme sprigs. Serve with the chermoula on the side.

YIELD: 2 SERVINGS

CHERMOULA

½ teaspoon cumin seeds

2 teaspoons coriander seeds

½ teaspoon Aleppo pepper

½ cup (48 g) chopped mint leaves

2 tablespoons (8 g) chopped Italian parsley

1 clove of garlic

½ teaspoon gros sel de Guérande or sea salt, plus more as needed

Juice from 1 lemon

½ cup (120 ml) olive oil

Grind the cumin and coriander seeds in a spice or coffee grinder. Place the spices, herbs, garlic, salt, lemon juice, and olive oil in a mini food processor. Purée to a paste consistency. Adjust the seasoning as necessary. This can be made in advance.

YIELD: ⅔ CUP (160 ML)

IN THE KITCHEN

WINTER SAVORY

Winter savory is one of those herbs that I classify as grassy because I find it to be most delicious fresh. However, with its small green, shiny, spearlike leaves with a peppery, woodsy flavor and a hint of citrus, it has many attributes of a woody herb. Winter savory is stronger than summer savory and is often used as a substitute for thyme.

Winter savory (as well as summer savory) is often used in Mediterranean cooking. Both are prevalent in the south of France. The recipes in this book use winter savory.

PAIRINGS

Savory pairs well with proteins that you would use with thyme. It is particularly good with poultry and rabbit. However, savory also goes with lamb, pork, wild boar, beef, veal, duck, and goose. Winter savory is wonderful for flavoring marinades and is a good match for eggs.

Winter savory is delicious in creamy soups, ragouts, and bean dishes. It goes well with starchy foods—potatoes, risotto, pastas, rice, farro, polenta, and stuffings—and is excellent with shelling beans, fava beans, lima beans, peas, and lentils.

Vegetables with lemony tones, such as artichokes and asparagus, work well with winter savory. Provençal vegetables (onions, eggplants, tomatoes, summer squash, and peppers) also go well with winter savory. Winter vegetables, root vegetables, and tuber vegetables, such as Brussels sprouts, carrots, parsnips, celery root, Jerusalem artichokes, cabbage, endive, radicchio, winter squash, kale, and parsnips, also benefit from savory. A nice combination with winter savory is mushrooms, truffles, and shallots.

Savory pairs with fruit the same way thyme does. When it comes to desserts, minced winter savory is better with savory baked items than with sweet ones. For example, winter savory is a good addition to biscuits, popovers, or savory cakes and muffins. It can be used lightly in a poaching liquid for fruit.

Savory leaves are excellent in salads. Chopped, the leaves are a bright addition to condiments. Consider artichokes with savory aioli or an artichoke purée with savory. Savory pairs well with walnuts, pecans, hazelnuts, pine nuts, and almonds and is excellent in a pesto for fish.

In terms of dairy, it is often paired with goat cheese, poivre d'âne (a cheese found in the south of France), and kitchen cheeses. It goes well with cream and mayonnaise and makes a nice companion for olives, olive oil, capers, butters, and garlic.

Savory goes well with many other herbs, including basil, chives, lavender, mint, parsley, and thyme. Winter savory is often used in the herbes de Provence blend (page 162). Ground savory can be combined with salt with or without the addition of other herbs.

HOW TO USE

Savory leaves are used whole or chopped. The stems are not eaten because they tend to be woody. Savory is often used early in the cooking process as part of a bouquet garni. I like to use savory raw at the end of the cooking process. Strip the leaves from the stem and give them a couple of chops. Add the leaves to cheese, salad, salad dressing, dip, or herb butter.

CASSOULET WITH CHICKEN AND WINTER SAVORY

Cassoulet, from the Languedoc region of France, is one of my favorite dishes. It is made with navy beans, sausage, lard or pork rinds, duck or goose confit legs, and sometimes lamb. There are three types, depending on the meat variations (Castelnaudary, Carcassonne, and Toulouse). There must be a ratio of 70 percent beans/vegetable to 30 percent meat for it to be a true cassoulet. Traditions dictate how it is prepared and whether the gratin crust should be broken (and how many times). This version, using chicken, would certainly be viewed with suspicion in France. However, winter savory pairs well with beans and poultry, so it was only natural to introduce a simplified cassoulet. For a more "classic" cassoulet, use duck confit legs (page 62) instead of the chicken and more thyme than savory.

8 whole chicken legs

Kosher salt and freshly ground black pepper, as needed

2 pounds (900 g) dried navy or flageolet beans

2 teaspoons gros sel de Guérande or sea salt, plus more as needed

1 tomato

Olive oil, as needed

4 pork sausages or 1 kielbasa (Use Toulouse sausage if you can find it.)

6 cloves of garlic, minced

1 yellow onion, diced

2 carrots, diced

½ cup (120 ml) dry white wine

6 cups (1.4 L) quality chicken stock, plus more as needed

1 winter savory bouquet garni (winter savory sprigs, 2 bay leaves, Italian parsley, and thyme tied together)

2 cups (230 g) bread crumbs from a baguette or country bread

1 tablespoon (3 g) minced winter savory

1 tablespoon (4 g) Italian parsley

4 tablespoons (55 g) unsalted butter, melted

Season the chicken with kosher salt and pepper. Wrap in plastic wrap and place in the refrigerator overnight.

Place the beans in a stockpot and add water that comes 2 inches (5 cm) above the beans. Cover with a lid and let the beans soak overnight.

Drain the beans. Add fresh water and the sea salt and simmer for about 1 hour until the beans are al dente (partially cooked but still slightly hard). Drain.

Preheat the oven to 350°F (180°C, or gas mark 4). Remove the chicken from the refrigerator.

Place a small saucepan of water over high heat. Use a small knife to remove the stem from the tomato. Make an "X" in the skin at the bottom. Add to the water and blanch for 1 to 2 minutes. Remove the tomato from the water with tongs and let cool. Once cool enough to handle, peel off the wrinkled skin and discard. Cut the tomato in half, squeeze out the seeds, and remove and discard the stem. Chop the tomato and set aside.

Place a large 6- to 6½-quart (5.7 to 6.2 L) Dutch oven over medium heat. Once the pot is hot, add olive oil to coat the bottom. When the oil is hot, add the chicken and sausages and brown on all sides. You don't want to crowd the pan. Work in batches if necessary. Remove the chicken and sausages and set aside on a plate.

Add the garlic to pan and, once fragrant, add the onion and carrots. Cook until the carrots are soft and the onions are translucent. Add the tomato and cook until the vegetables are beginning to stick to the bottom of the pan. Add the wine, scraping up the bits from the bottom of the pan. Cook until the wine has been cooked out of the pan. Turn off the heat.

Add half of the beans to the pot along with the sausage. Cover with the rest of the beans. Add the chicken stock and bouquet garni. Cover with the lid or aluminum foil, transfer to the oven, and cook for about 1 hour, stirring occasionally.

Insert the chicken into the beans and continue to cook for another hour. (If you cook the chicken too long, the chicken bones may loosen and come apart. If they do, be careful when serving.) Cassoulet should be creamy; add more stock if necessary. Remove from the oven; remove and discard the bouquet garni.

Combine the bread crumbs, herbs, and butter in a bowl. Spread the mixture over the top of the cassoulet. Return it to the oven, without the lid, and bake until crispy, 5 to 7 minutes. Remove from the oven and let cool slightly before serving, at least 30 minutes. If you have any leftovers, the cassoulet tastes even better the next day.

....

YIELD: 12 SERVINGS

WINTER SAVORY TARTS

These tartlets make a lovely starter. This recipe makes four starter course tarts or nine smaller tarts to use as something to accompany an aperitif.

5 ounces (140 g) goat cheese

2 tablespoons (5 g) chopped winter savory leaves

1 (9 x 9-inch, or 23 x 23 cm) sheet frozen puff pastry, defrosted in the refrigerator

1 tablespoon (15 ml) olive oil

4 cloves of garlic, minced

3 cups (480 g) thinly sliced shallots

1 tablespoon (15 g) brown sugar

Pinch of kosher salt

2 teaspoons white wine

1 egg, beaten

⅓ cup (33 g) pitted Niçoise olives, for garnish

Thyme leaves, for garnish

Preheat the oven to 400°F (200°C, or gas mark 6). Line a rimmed baking sheet with parchment paper.

Combine the goat cheese and savory leaves in a small bowl. Set aside.

On a lightly floured surface, use a rolling pin to roll out puff pastry to remove any folds. Use a knife or pizza cutter to cut the pastry dough into 4 squares, approximately 4 x 4 inches (10 x 10 cm), or 9 smaller squares for appetizer-size tarts. Place the pastry squares on the prepared baking sheet. Use a fork to poke a few holes in the pastry squares. Gently spread the goat cheese–herb mixture on each square (about ⅛ inch [3 mm] thick) in the center, stopping ½ to ¾ inch (1.3 to 2 cm) from the edge of the square. Place the baking sheet with the pastry squares in the refrigerator to keep cold.

Heat the olive oil in a sauté pan and add the garlic. Sauté until fragrant, 30 seconds to 1 minute, and then add the shallots and cook until tender, 10 to 12 minutes. Add the sugar and salt and stir to combine. When the shallots begin to stick to the pan, add the wine. Cook until the wine evaporates, 2 minutes. Remove the pan from the heat and set aside.

Remove the baking sheet from the refrigerator. Brush the beaten egg on the uncovered portions of the pastry squares. Add the shallots on top of the goat cheese. Place the baking sheet with the pastry squares in the oven. Bake for 10 to 12 minutes until puffed and golden brown. Remove from the oven. Garnish with the olives and tender thyme leaves.

YIELD: 4 STARTER COURSE TARTS OR 9 APPETIZER TARTS

ROASTED NEW POTATOES WITH SPLIT GARLIC

Roasted potatoes are an easy side that pairs nicely with most meats and salads. The combination of thyme and savory is a common herb pairing and here it brings a freshness to the baby potatoes and shallots. The incorporation of roasted whole garlic adds a little sweetness. Use shallots that are the same size as the potatoes.

2 pounds (900 g) new potatoes	¼ cup (10 g) winter savory leaves
16 cloves of garlic	Olive oil, as needed
16 shallots, peeled	1 teaspoon gros sel de Guérande or sea salt
8 sprigs of thyme	Freshly ground black pepper, as needed

Preheat the oven to 375°F (190°C, or gas mark 5).

Cut the potatoes in half. (They should all be roughly the same size.) Split the garlic cloves by making a cut in the outside skin. Don't peel. Combine the potatoes, garlic, shallots, thyme, and savory in a bowl, drizzle with olive oil, and toss to coat. Sprinkle with salt and pepper. Place in a baking dish.

Roast until the potatoes are tender and the outsides are crispy, 30 to 40 minutes. Check them every 10 to 15 minutes and move the potatoes around so they don't stick on the bottom of the baking dish.

YIELD: 6 TO 8 SERVINGS

◀ *Winter Savory Tarts, page 160*

IN THE KITCHEN

HERB COMBINATIONS

Herbs are often best used in combination with one another. There are two classic combinations that are used so often they deserve a special mention.

Fines herbes (*fines* is pronounced FEEN) is the classic combination of chervil, chives, parsley, and tarragon in equal proportions. These herbs are used fresh, not dried, because their value is in their freshness. Dried, they are worthless green dust.

Fines herbes are particularly wonderful with green salads, eggs, root vegetables, spring vegetables, seafood, and fish, including delicate fish.

Herbes de Provence is not a set combination; you will see many variations. Generally, herbes de Provence includes the herbs growing wild in the French countryside: French lavender, French thyme, and rosemary. Savory, bay laurel, parsley, and fennel seeds are often included (sometimes all of these are added).

Herbes de Provence is used both dried and fresh. This chapter has a recipe for the fresh version, but the dried version is most common. Dried, the combination is an easy boost for roasting meats, such as lamb, wild boar, and poultry. You can use the herbs on the skin of the meat, mixed in butter and spread on the skin (best for poultry), or even ground with sea salt. You can also roast meat and fish directly on the fresh herbs.

In the summer in the south of France, where lavender, fennel, and thyme grow along the roadside and rosemary, basil, and savory thrive under the Provençal sun, I use these herbs fresh in vegetable farces and ragouts typical of the region: tomatoes, zucchini, eggplant, and onions.

FINES HERBES QUICHE WITH FLOWERS

Quiche is a savory, baked custard in a shell. As my children say, it is "egg pie." The point of fines herbes is the freshness it brings, so I include only light spring onions and zucchini and omit heavy vegetables and cheese. However, with the buttery, light crust, it still tastes like a (savory egg) pie. Use a 9-inch (23 cm) tart pan with a removable bottom for the prettiest presentation.

FOR CRUST:

2½ cups (313 g) sifted all-purpose flour

1¼ teaspoons kosher salt

2 large eggs

7 tablespoons (98 g) unsalted butter, ice cold and cubed

2 tablespoons (28 ml) ice cold water

FOR FILLING:

4 large eggs, beaten

½ cup (120 ml) heavy cream

½ cup (120 ml) low-fat milk

1 tablespoon (14 g) crème fraîche

Pinch of freshly ground black pepper

½ teaspoon kosher salt

1 tablespoon (1.9 g) minced chervil

1 tablespoon (4 g) minced Italian parsley

1 tablespoon (3 g) minced chives

1 tablespoon (4 g) minced tarragon

1 tablespoon (14 g) unsalted butter

½ cup (50 g) thinly sliced spring onions

1 cup (120 g) sliced baby zucchini

Organic broccoli flowers, chives flowers, zucchini blossoms, or marigold petals, for garnish

To make the crust: Combine the flour and salt in a food processor. Add the eggs and pulse to combine. Add the butter cubes and pulse until incorporated. The mixture will have coarse chunks. Drizzle in the cold water until the dough just comes together. Don't overprocess. Pat the dough into a disk and wrap in plastic. Refrigerate for 30 minutes. The dough can be made in advance.

Preheat the oven to 350°F (180°C, or gas mark 4).

On a floured surface, use a rolling pin to roll out the dough into a circle ⅛ inch (3 mm) thick. Fold the dough over the rolling pin and carefully place in a 9-inch (23 cm) tart pan. Press the dough into the pan and roll the pin over the top of the pan to cut the dough against the edges of the pan. Pierce the bottom of the dough in several places with a fork. Gently cover the dough with a generous piece of aluminum foil and place pie weights or dried beans on top of the foil. Place the pan on a rimmed baking sheet and bake for about 5 minutes until the shape is set. Remove the weights and aluminum foil. Continue to bake the tart shell empty for about 7 minutes until the crust no longer looks wet but has no color. Remove from the oven and let it cool.

To make the filling: Combine the eggs, cream, milk, crème fraîche, pepper, and salt in a bowl. Combine the herbs in a separate bowl.

Place a sauté pan over medium heat and add the butter. Once the butter is melted, add the onions and zucchini. Turn the heat to low and place a piece of aluminum foil over the zucchini and onions; press down so the zucchini stays flat. Cook for 5 to 7 minutes until the vegetables are cooked through but not browned. Remove from the heat.

Spread the zucchini and onions over the bottom of the crust. Spread the herbs on top. Gently pour the egg mixture over. Place the quiche on a baking sheet and bake for 25 to 30 minutes. The quiche is done when the crust edges are golden brown in color and the eggs are set and slightly puffed.

Garnish with the fresh flowers in a decorative way.

YIELD: ONE 9-INCH (23 CM) QUICHE

STUFFED TOMATOES À LA PROVENÇALE ET MAROC

With vegetables à la Provençale, onions, tomatoes, and zucchini are often stuffed with a farce (stuffing) made of ground veal or beef and sometimes bread crumbs or rice with herbs, onion, and garlic. My version combines fresh herbes de Provence with a Moroccan influence. It is like a tagine in a tomato farce. A tagine usually includes merguez (a spicy lamb sausage), chicken, tomatoes, onions, herbs, and some type of dried fruit. If you are able to find merguez sausage, omit the seasoning because the sausage is already heavily spiced. If you are using ground lamb and want the couscous spicier, serve a little harissa on the side.

6 tomatoes

¼ teaspoon kosher salt, plus more as needed

3 tablespoons (27 g) pine nuts

½ cup (88 g) uncooked couscous

8 ounces (225 g) ground lamb

½ teaspoon piment d'espelette

⅛ teaspoon ground cumin

1 or 2 pinches of cayenne

Freshly ground black pepper, as needed

Olive oil, as needed

2 cloves of garlic, minced

¼ cup (40 g) small diced yellow onion

1 tablespoon (9 g) dried currants

½ teaspoon finely minced rosemary

1 tablespoon (2 g) thyme leaves, plus more for garnish

2 teaspoons chopped savory leaves

1 tablespoon (4 g) chopped Italian parsley, plus more for garnish

Preheat the oven to 375°F (190°C, or gas mark 5). Line a baking sheet with parchment paper.

Cut the tops off the tomatoes and set aside. Hollow out the tomatoes. Strain the flesh, discarding the seeds and the tomato water, and chop and reserve. Sprinkle the interiors of the tomatoes and the flesh side of the tops with salt, as needed, to draw the moisture out. Place the tomatoes upside down on the prepared baking sheet and set aside.

Place the pine nuts in a pan over medium heat. Toast until lightly brown and the nuts begin to release their oils. Spread on a plate to cool.

Cook the couscous according to the package instructions. Cover with a lid to keep warm.

In a bowl, combine the ground lamb with the piment d'espelette, cumin, cayenne, and black pepper. Place a frying pan over medium heat. Add a few tablespoons (45 ml) of olive oil to the pan. Once the oil is warm, add the lamb. If you want to taste the seasoning, cook 1 tablespoon (15 g) of the mixture first and make seasoning adjustments as needed (but remember that you want it to be spicy because when combined with the couscous, it will be much milder). Place the rest of the ground lamb in the pan. Break it up with a wooden spoon and cook until no longer pink. Remove the lamb and set aside in a bowl.

Return the pan to the stove. Add the garlic and once fragrant, add the onion and then the reserved chopped tomatoes. Cook until the moisture has been cooked out of the tomatoes, at least 5 minutes. Turn off the heat. Incorporate the tomato mixture into the lamb along with the pine nuts and currants. Fluff the couscous with a fork and add to the meat. Place in a bowl and mix in the herbs. Adjust the seasoning to taste.

Rub the tomato skins lightly with olive oil, stuff with the couscous mixture, and place the tomato tops on top of the mixture. Place in a baking dish and bake for 10 to 15 minutes until the skins begin to wrinkle slightly.

Garish with the thyme and parsley leaves. Serve warm.

YIELD: 6 SERVINGS

FINES HERBES GREEN HERB SUMMER SALAD

Light, green foods are wonderful with a fines herbes combination. Tart green apples and al dente asparagus are two examples. Crottin de chèvre is a goat's milk cheese that is often served warm on toast points with a green salad in the south of France. This a variation of that dish.

1 bunch asparagus (about 10 ounces, or 280 g)	2 teaspoons minced Italian parsley
1 tablespoon (15 ml) Champagne or red wine vinegar	2 teaspoons minced tarragon leaves
1 teaspoon finely minced shallot	½ of a Granny Smith apple, cut into julienne
3 tablespoons (45 ml) quality olive oil or truffle oil	1 handful of mâche
Gros sel de Guérande or sea salt, as needed	2 handfuls of wild arugula
2 teaspoons minced chervil	4 slices of sandwich bread
2 teaspoons minced chives	4 ounces (115 g) crottin de chèvre cheese, sliced

Preheat the broiler or toaster oven.

Trim the asparagus by breaking off the fibrous bottoms. Peel the exterior of the stalk 1 inch (2.5 cm) below the spear. Cut the stalks into pieces 3 to 4 inches (7.5 to 10 cm) in length.

Bring a saucepan of salted water to a boil. Blanch the asparagus stalks for 2 to 3 minutes; they should still be bright green and crisp to the tooth. Remove the asparagus and place in an ice bath. Once cool, set on paper towels to dry.

Place the vinegar in a bowl. Whisk in the oil and season with salt to taste. Add the shallots.

In a large bowl, combine the asparagus, herbs, apple, and greens. Slowly add the dressing and toss gently to coat. Divide among 4 plates.

Cut the crusts off of the bread slices. Cut the squares into 2 triangles. Place a slice of goat cheese on each triangle. Place on a baking sheet and place under the broiler to toast the bread and warm the cheese. Place 2 toast points alongside each salad. Serve immediately, while the cheese is warm.

YIELD: 4 SERVINGS

ACKNOWLEDGMENTS

How does one trace back the roots of a passion? My love of herbs and herb gardening was probably first nurtured by the women I met growing up in my parents' rural California home. From them, I discovered what happens when seeds are planted, how to manage water, why weeds cannot be ignored, and a host of other basic gardening skills.

Later, when I planted my first herb garden, those early lessons surfaced and I was off on my own gardening adventures. Since then, I have learned much and made it my mission to teach others about gardening for flavor, fragrance, and the unbridled joy of digging in the dirt. My love of herb gardening will continue to provide me with these and many other good things for the rest of my life, just as it did for those women who taught me about their passion many years ago.

—AM

I would like to thank Tiffany Hill, for reaching out to me with this project, and my editor April White, for seeing the project through to completion. A special thank you to photographer Alan de Herrera for his time and talent. I would like to thank everyone at Quarry who worked on this project, including Anne Re, and, of course, my co-author Ann McCormick, who inspired me to make my thumb a little greener.

Thank you to my beautiful family and friends for their patience with my schedule and their unfailing support. Finally, a big thank you to my wonderful daughters, who inspire me each day.

—LBM

ABOUT THE AUTHORS

LISA BAKER MORGAN

Chef Morgan is a private chef and a graduate of the Le Cordon Bleu College of Culinary Arts in Los Angeles. Inspired to share her love and knowledge of food with others, this former civil trial attorney combined her communication skills gained as a lawyer with her passion for cooking and began providing cooking classes in 2009. She has taught in both Los Angeles and France.

In 2010, Chef Morgan began the food/travel blog "à table." She has written hundreds of original recipes and continues to publish original recipes on her site.

In 2011, Chef Morgan published her first cookbook, *Simple Pleasures: Fifty-Two Weeks of Turning Ordinary Ingredients into Extraordinary Moments*. In 2012, Chef Morgan was featured in the book *The Mothers of Reinvention* (Vanguard Press).

Chef Morgan's cooking style reflects both her culinary training and her personal life. She divides her time between her homes in Los Angeles and Paris. A marathon runner and mother of two daughters, she emphasizes lighter, healthier preparations using seasonal, quality ingredients. To follow Chef Morgan, visit her site www.chefmorgan.com and find her on Facebook at facebook.com/cheflisabakermorgan.

ANN MCCORMICK

If you enjoy herbs and organic gardening, you'll want to meet Ann McCormick, the Herb 'n Cowgirl. A lifelong gardener, she has devoted her time since 1998 to writing and speaking about her favorite subject. Ann is a columnist for *Herb Quarterly*, contributes to various regional and national home and garden and lifestyle magazines, and blogs from her website, www.herbncowgirl.com. The Herb 'n Cowgirl also shares her love of herbs and her gardening techniques as a speaker and media guest.

RESOURCES

IN THE GARDEN
BOOKS
Better Homes and Gardens Herb Gardening. Des Moines, IA: Meredith Corporation, 2012.

Bown, Deni. *Herbal: The Essential Guide to Herbs for Living*. London: Pavilion Books Ltd., 2003.

Creasy, Rosalind. *Edible Landscaping*. San Francisco, CA: Sierra Club Books, 2010.

Gips, Kathleen. *Flora's Dictionary: The Victorian Language of Herbs and Flowers*. Chagrin Falls, OH: Village Herb Shop, Inc., 1995.

Hill, Madalene, Gwen Barclay, and Jean Hardy. *Southern Herb Growing*. Fredericksburg, TX: Shearer Publishing, 1987.

McVicar, Jekka. *Grow Herbs: An Inspiring Guide to Growing and Using Herbs*. New York: DK Publishing Inc., 2010.

Simmons, Adelma Grenier. *Herb Gardening in Five Seasons*. New York: D. Van Nostrand Company, Inc., 1964.

Staub, Jack. *75 Exceptional Herbs for Your Garden*. Layton, UT: Gibbs Smith, 2008.

Tucker, Arthur O., and Thomas DeBaggio. *The Big Book of Herbs: A Comprehensive Illustrated Reference to Herbs of Flavor and Fragrance*. U.S.A.: Interweave Press, 2000.

ORGANIZATIONS
The Herb Society of Great Britain: www.herbsociety.org.uk

International Herb Association: www.iherb.org

IN THE KITCHEN
BOOKS AND MAGAZINES
Dornenburg, Andrew, and Karen Page. *Culinary Artistry*. Malden, MA: John Wiley & Sons, 1996.

Librairie Larousse. *Larousse Gastronomique: The World's Greatest Culinary Encyclopedia*. New York: Clarkson Potter, 2001.

Malouf, Greg, and Lucy Malouf. *Artichoke to Za'atar*. Oakland, CA: University of California Press, 2008.

McGee, Harold. *On Food and Cooking: The Science and Lore of the Kitchen*. Revised updated edition. New York: Scribner, 2004.

Page, Karen, and Andrew Dornenburg. *The Flavor Bible*. New York: Little, Brown & Company, 2008.

Saveurs: Le Magazine de l'Art de Vivre Gourmand: www.editions-burda.fr/saveurs.

Thorens, Thierry. *Le Goût des Fleurs*. Paris: Actes Sud, 2009.

Zeste: Cuisinons Simple et Bon: www.cotemaison.fr/kiosque/kiosquezeste.asp.

SPECIALTY PRODUCTS
Salt

Gros sel de Guérande: www.seldeguerande.com

Le Saunier de Camargue fleur de sel: www.walmart.com and www.surlatable.com

Mustard

Maille Moutarde a l'Ancienne: www.maille.com

Moutarde de Normandie Toustain-Barville: www.toustain-barville.com

Vinegar

Balsamic Cream Terre Bormane, Crema a Base di "Aceto Balsamico di Modena IGP": www.bienmanger.com

Edmund de Vin Rouge Aromatisé à la Figue: www.epicuriensdefrance.com

Olive Oil

Huile d'Olive, La Moulin a Huile d'Aureille, Vallée de Baux de Provence AOP: www.moulin-aureille.com

Huile d'Olive, Moulin du Mas des Barres AOP: www.aoc-lesbauxdeprovence.com

Baking Supplies

Bob Red Mill's oat flour: www.bobsredmill.com

King Arthur all-purpose flour: www.kingarthurflour.com

Nielsen-Massey Madagascar Bourbon Pure Vanilla Bean Paste: www.nielsenmassey.com

Miscellaneous

Piment d'espelette: www.amazon.com

Rendered duck fat: www.hudsonvalleyfoiegras.com

INDEX